# Quaint Birdhouses
## You Can Paint and Decorate

Dorothy Egan

**NORTH LIGHT BOOKS**
CINCINNATI, OHIO

**Quaint Birdhouses You Can Paint and Decorate.** Copyright © 2000 by Dorothy Egan. Manufactured in China. All rights reserved. The patterns and drawings in this book are for the personal use of the reader. By permission of the author and publisher, they may be either hand-traced or photocopied to make single copies, but under no circumstances may they be resold or republished. It is permissible for the purchaser to reproduce the designs contained herein and sell them at fairs, bazaars and craft shows.

No other part of this book may be reproduced in any form or by any electronic or mechanical means including information storage and retrieval systems without permission in writing from the publisher, except by a reviewer, who may quote brief passages in a review. Published by North Light Books, an imprint of F&W Publications, Inc., 1507 Dana Avenue, Cincinnati, Ohio 45207. (800) 289-0963. First edition.

Other fine North Light Books are available from your local bookstore, art supply store or direct from the publisher.

04 03 02 01 00     5 4 3 2 1

**Library of Congress Cataloging-in-Publication Data**

Egan, Dorothy.
   Quaint birdhouses you can paint and decorate / [Dorothy Egan].
   p.   cm.
   ISBN 0-89134-986-3 (pbk. : alk. paper)
   1. Painting.  2. Decoration and ornament.  3. Birdhouses.  I. Title
TT385.E35  2000
745.7'23–dc21

                                                                                   99-36672
                                                                                   CIP

Editor: Jane Friedman
Designer: Mary Barnes Clark
Production artist: Kathy Gardner
Production coordinator: John Peavler
Photographer: Christine Polomsky

# About the Author

Dorothy Egan, author of *Painting and Decorating Birdhouses*, has been involved with painting and the craft industry for most of her life. Her artistic career began as a matter of economy, as she restored old furniture and found creative ways to decorate her home on a newlywed's budget. Dorothy began to share her talents with friends and was soon earning extra money by selling her projects in consignment shops and at craft shows. After taking decorative painting classes, she began to teach at a local tole shop. Since then, Dorothy has produced or co-produced more than thirty books, is a regular contributor to several magazines, and has conducted painting seminars throughout the United States and Canada.

# Table of Contents

# Introduction

People have been fascinated with birds almost as long as there has been recorded history. During the Victorian era, birdhouses were brought indoors and their elaborate construction and decorations made them a popular new decorating trend. Over the years, they have remained of major interest to woodworkers and birdwatchers, but in recent years, they have once again become a popular decorating accessory. They are found throughout many gardens, on patios and porches, but many of them are used indoors and are never intended for use by live birds. They are made to fill a creative urge and to be enjoyed throughout the year, bringing a sense of nature and tranquility into homes.

This book takes that idea a step further by showing you how to create a whole village of birdhouses. The patterns and techniques given can be easily adapted to other styles of birdhouses. The same design elements can be used on birdhouses that are different shapes and sizes. There are several examples of how the same house can look totally different by adding architectural details, using different painting styles and techniques or adding miniature accessories.

There are tips on how to use simple, readily available items as tools to create a variety of textures and finishes. These projects will show you how inexpensive supplies from craft stores and home improvement stores can add charm and interest to an ordinary commercial birdhouse. This book may also inspire you to create your own styles. Hopefully, it will lead you into a world of fun and fulfillment by guiding you along the path of creativity.

# General Instructions

Because some techniques and supplies are repeated on a number of the designs, this section gives you general information about getting started and helpful hints to remember as you work on individual projects.

The following steps for preparing a birdhouse for painting and decorating are basic and are used on most of the houses. These steps will not be repeated in the individual instructions, but any variations from these steps will be noted.

## Filling Nail Holes

To achieve a smooth, undimpled finish and to ensure that the metallic surfaces of the nailheads do not show, all nails should be countersunk and the holes filled with a commercial wood filler. Many ready-made houses are put together with staples that should also be covered.

***Countersink nails.*** Use a nail set to countersink nails so that the heads will not show on the finished birdhouse.

***Apply wood filler.*** Fill the nail holes with a commercial wood filler. Apply the filler with putty or a painting knife, slightly overfilling the hole. Allow it to dry before sanding. J.W. etc. wood filler was used for the projects in this book because it sands easily and accepts paint and stain well.

## Sanding

Most commercial birdhouses need to be sanded, as shipping and climate changes may cause rough spots on the surface. Using plain sandpaper is effective and inexpensive. Begin with a medium grit to smooth the roughest spots, then use a fine or extrafine grit for the final sanding. Always sand with the grain of the wood, not across it. Pay close attention to splintered or rough edges. Sanding blocks are available and are easier to hold, so they make the job a little faster. A small electric vibrating sander, called a palm sander, is probably the quickest and easiest way to prepare the house for painting, but it is the most expensive, so it is only practical if you already own one. If you plan to do a lot of woodworking, it is a wise investment.

A project can be sanded after it has been painted, removing paint from edges and areas that would receive the most wear, to heighten the aged effect.

*Basic sanding.* Sand the birdhouse well, removing any rough spots and excess wood filler.

*Electric sanding.* A small electric palm sander is easy to use and makes quick work of smoothing the wood.

*Aging.* To create a more primitive, well-worn look, use a wood rasp or coarse sandpaper to round sharp edges.

# Other Preparations

*Wipe with a tack cloth.* After sanding, always wipe the surface with a tack cloth before sealing or painting. A tack cloth is an inexpensive treated cloth with a slight stickiness that picks up fine dust particles, which cause unattractive roughness in the finish. Tack cloths are available where painting supplies are sold.

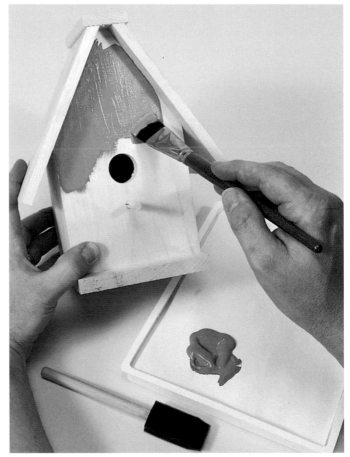

*Basecoating.* Basecoating means applying a smooth, even coat of paint over a surface. This paint will act as a background for further decorative work. Remember several light coats are better than one heavy coat. Bottled acrylic paints were used on the projects in this book. These paints come in a wide variety of colors, are readily available and easy to use, clean up with soap and water and are very durable. The brands and colors listed in the individual instructions are merely suggestions. If you don't have the exact color listed, use the photograph as a guide. Colors can also be changed to fit your personal taste or decorating theme.

*Sealing.* Although basecoating with a good acrylic paint is often sufficient to seal the wood, using a commercial sealer makes painting easier and further protects the wood if the house will be used outdoors. Wood that is to be stained rather than painted should be sealed so the stain will be absorbed more evenly. Make sure you allow the sealer to dry, then sand lightly and wipe with a tack cloth. The projects in this book were sealed with Designs From the Heart sealer, but there are many good sealers on the market. Avoid sealers that cause the grain to swell and become slightly rough. Ask your local craft supply dealer to recommend one.

## Transferring a Pattern

Several of the projects in this book include a black-and-white pattern. Use these patterns as a guideline to freehand the designs on your project, or transfer the pattern directly to your surface. To transfer a pattern, lay a piece of tracing paper directly on the pattern and trace over it with a black pen. Flip the tracing paper face down and trace over the back of the design with pencil or chalk, using a color that will show over your basecoat or surface color. Then position your pattern face-up on your project, and trace the pen lines with a stylus or dried-out ball-point pen, which will transfer the chalk or pencil pattern onto the surface.

## Locating Raw Birdhouses

Commercial preassembled, ready-to-decorate birdhouses are widely available at craft and hobby stores. Flea and craft markets are another good source of pre-made birdhouses, often providing unique shapes and personalized designs. Those with woodworking skills will enjoy building their own birdhouses to decorate. If you are unable to locate the style of birdhouse you need for any of the following projects, see page 126 for a complete list of the suppliers used in this book.

## Brushes

Use a good-quality brush or sponge brush. Many inexpensive synthetic brushes are available that wear well and are designed for decorative painting. The brush sizes listed in the instructions are guidelines—a larger or smaller size may feel more comfortable for you.

Stencil brush

Liner brush

Round brush

Sponge brush

Flat brush

## Other Finishes and Techniques

Many other finishing techniques, such as crackled, sponged or spattered finishes, are mentioned in the projects. There are helpful hints mentioned in the instructions, but the following information is basic to each particular technique. A special study of crackling is on page 86.

### Sponging

Many of the projects included in this book have some sponging in the basic techniques. Most of them were done with ordinary upholstery foam. It is available in most fabric stores. It is also occasionally used for packing. It is soft so it does not need to be moistened before using and is so inexpensive that it can be thrown away after use.

Sea sponges create a larger, more distinct pattern than foam. They should be dipped in water and squeezed dry before use.

***Sponging With Foam.*** Squeeze paint onto the palette. Cut a 2-inch square of foam. Pull corners up to form a pouf. Dip the pouf into the first color. Pat it on the palette to remove excess and distribute the paint evenly. Pat the paint onto the surface until you achieve the desired coverage, refilling the sponge as needed.

***Adding Texture.*** Repeat process with second color, sponging over, but not covering the first application of paint.

Quaint Birdhouses You Can Paint and Decorate

**Using a third color.** Apply the third color in the same way. The final color should finish covering the surface, but colors may look spotty and underblended.

**Blending with a sponge.** Use a dry-wiped sponge to blend and soften colors. If needed for extra blending or to strengthen primary color, reapply any color and blend again.

**Using a sea sponge.** For a more distinct sponged pattern, use a natural sea sponge to apply paint. Wet the sponge, then squeeze it as dry as possible before dipping it into the paint.

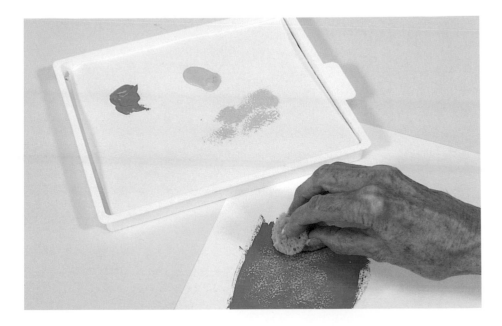

## Spattering

If you have not used this technique, it's always a good idea to test the effect on paper before you use it on a finished project. To spatter the project, dip a stiff bristle brush into thinned paint. Holding the brush six to eight inches from the surface, drag a painting knife across the bristles toward you. The amount of water used to thin the paint and distance between the brush and the surface will cause variations in the size and boldness of the spattering. Let dry before applying a finish.

## Painting Shingles

The basic technique for painting a shingled roof is to first establish the horizontal rows of shingles by drawing them lightly with a pencil. Establish shading under each row with a dark value, and highlight the bottom edges of the shingles with a light value. Use a liner brush with thinned paint, usually the shading color, to outline the rows with slightly squiggly, irregular lines. Draw a few vertical lines to indicate individual shingles. The shading and highlighting can be done with a flat brush, fan brush, rake brush or sponge to create different effects. Specific suggestions are in the individual instructions.

Quick shingle work can be done by double-loading a piece of upholstery foam to pat the rows of shingles. Afterwards, loosely outline the rows with a liner brush. See page 63–64 for an example.

## Creating Bricks

Before starting, tape off the house using ½-inch-wide masking tape to create the lines of mortar between the bricks. Work one side of the house at a time. Starting at the bottom, place one strip of tape across the side of the house. Leave approximately a ¹⁄₁₆-inch-space and place another strip above the first one. Repeat until the side of the house is covered.

***Paint the mortar lines.*** Use a foam pouf to pat the mortar color over the openings between the strips of tape. Remove the tape.

***Reapply tape.*** When the paint is dry, apply the tape again so that the open lines fall halfway between the first lines. This will create mortar lines in between the first ones. Sponge the open lines and remove the tape.

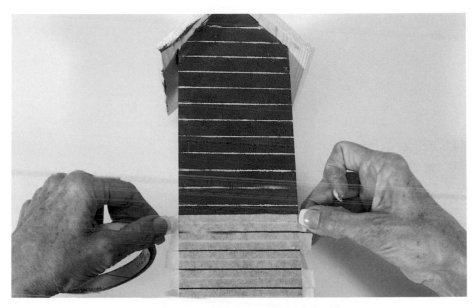

***Paint vertical mortar lines.*** Use a liner brush to paint the vertical lines of mortar. Remember to alternate lines on each row.

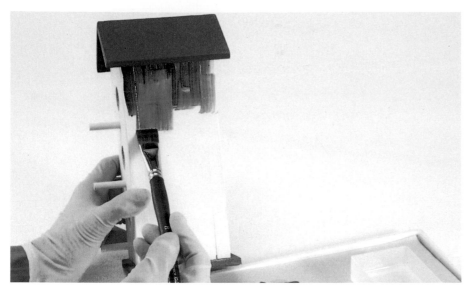

Apply thinned oil, acrylic paints or commercially prepared glazes to the surface of the birdhouse with a brush.

The surface should be completely covered with the antiquing glaze.

## Antiquing

Antiquing is the process of adding a glaze of brown or black paint over a finished surface to produce an aged, slightly dulled effect. Although antiquing is suggested for some projects, you may decide you like the brighter, newer look of undulled paint and choose not to antique, or you may prefer to antique all of your projects to add a "historical" character. Since antiquing is a matter of personal preference, complete instructions and materials are listed in this section rather than within each project.

There are several methods of antiquing. The houses in this book were done with oil paints thinned with a few drops of odor-free thinner. Oils are inexpensive and versatile, because several colors can be mixed together to create a glaze that is just right for the base color used. For example, Burnt Umber may be too red in tone and Raw Umber too brown, but if they are mixed together, they make a warm, neutral antiquing color. Burnt Umber and black is another good combination. These oil colors can also be used as a wood stain.

Acrylics can be thinned with gel or blending medium to create a glaze, although it is harder to achieve even coverage with this method. Premixed oil- and

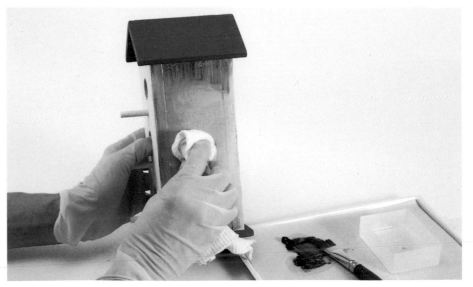

Wipe away excess antiquing with a soft, dry cloth.

### Antiquing Materials

- oil paints, such as Raw Umber, Burnt Umber, Raw Sienna and/or black
- odorless thinner
- *or* commercial antiquing glaze
- *or* acrylic paint in above colors and a blending medium
- flat synthetic brush
- soft, lint-free cloth
- small flat brush
- commercial varnish

Quaint Birdhouses You Can Paint and Decorate

water-based glazes are also available in craft stores, paint stores and home improvement departments.

Antique after the entire project is painted and dry. A light coat of varnish will make the glaze easier to control and make it easier to create a soft, even effect. Applying the glaze to an unvarnished piece will result in a heavier, more rustic effect. Apply the glaze with a brush, then wipe away excess with a soft, lint-free cloth, wiping in a circular motion to prevent lines and streaks.

Use a soft, dry brush to remove glaze from hard-to-reach places. Wipe with a soft cloth or brush dampened with thinner to remove more glaze for a subtle effect or to create areas of highlight. Antiquing should be allowed to dry thoroughly before the final finish is applied.

If you like the effect you've achieved, stop here and let it dry.

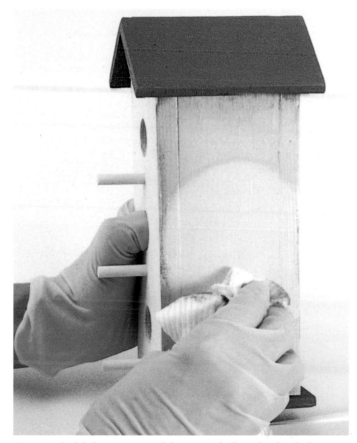

To create highlights or a very subtle antiqued effect, dip the cloth into thinner and rub the surface to remove more glaze.

Use a small brush to apply and remove antiquing in hard-to-reach places.

## Varnishing

Finish your birdhouse with a good quality varnish, using a wide flat brush or sponge brush. Where you plan to display the house will determine the type of varnish used. A house that is purely decorative could be finished with a water-based brush-on varnish, while one that will be used outdoors would need to be finished with a product especially for indoor/outdoor use. Read labels or consult your local paint store for advice.

Spray varnishes are another option. They are easy to use and require no brush cleaning but are considerably more expensive if you plan to do several birdhouses. Apply spray varnish outdoors. Hold the surface to be sprayed horizontally to prevent runs and the can several inches away to achieve a light, even mist. Several thin coats are better than one heavy coat. Be sure to cover all the areas of the birdhouse.

## Other Finishes

Other finishing techniques used in this book, such as crackling and texturing, may be applied to any style of birdhouse and used in any project. Experiment with these techniques to create a birdhouse that is very personally yours.

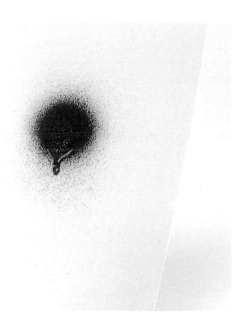

*Wrong way*

*Right way*

Quaint Birdhouses You Can Paint and Decorate

# Additions, Attachments, Accessories

## Cutting Craft Sticks

Many of the projects include craft sticks (Popsicle sticks) and jumbo craft sticks in the supply lists. The easiest and most exact way to cut the sticks is with a jigsaw or band saw, but they can also be cut with pruning shears, old heavy-duty scissors or a craft knife. Fiskars pruning shears are a good size and shape for this purpose. Sand the ends of the sticks to a smooth finish.

## Adhesives

The types of adhesives used on the birdhouse depend on the type of use it will have. Most of the wood pieces are attached with ordinary thick white craft glue. Wood glue is also suitable. The accessories in these projects were attached with either white craft glue or a glue gun. If the house is to be used outdoors, clear silicone sealant is an excellent adhesive that holds up well when exposed to the elements.

## Accessorizing

Don't just paint the windows and doors on the house—make real ones! Using craft sticks, balsa strips and wood cutouts adds not only interest to your birdhouse, but also dimension.

Look for miniatures at craft stores that might fit your theme, or make your own with polymer clay.

Architectural interest is easy to accomplish with simple wood chimneys, bell towers and window sashes. Experiment with roof and siding treatments also. Flat wood surfaces are easily transformed with creative uses of mortar patch, small twigs or corrugated cardboard.

*T*his first project reveals the creative potential of optional trims and small additions. Make this charming, very dependable looking bank building by adding texture with ready-mixed mortar patch and bricks made from basswood strips.

VILLAGE BANK

Quaint Birdhouses You Can Paint and Decorate

# Bank

## 1 Preparation

Sand the roof and the base. Wipe with a tack cloth to remove dust particles.

Transform the character of a plain, mass-produced birdhouse with imaginative trims: Use welded wire for the window, a cardboard cutout for the door and ordinary beads for urns.

## 2 Make the Bricks

Paint the ¼-inch wide basswood strips with Red Iron Oxide, then randomly brush them with tints of Brandy Wine and touches of Midnight Blue, adding only enough color variation to give a bricklike appearance. Do not overblend. When strips are dry, use a craft knife or pruning shears to cut them into ⅜-inch and ½-inch lengths, approximately fifty of each size. Touch up the ends with Red Iron Oxide.

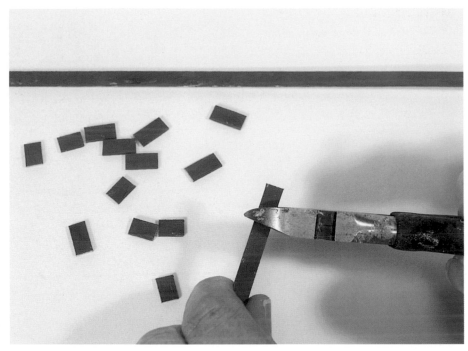

Cut the painted basswood strips into ⅜-inch and ½-inch lengths.

## 3 Glue the Bricks to the House

Beginning on the front of the house, ¾-inch from the bottom, glue bricks along the front edge of the house, alternating the sizes. Let them overhang the side edge slightly. Stop ¾-inch from the top. Cut a length of craft stick ⅛-inch shorter than the space between the base and the bricks. Glue it underneath the bottom brick. Cut a ⅝-inch piece of ⅛-inch square basswood strip. Glue it between the craft stick and the base. Repeat above the bricks, under the eaves. Paint the wood pieces above and below the bricks with Titanium White. Repeat all steps on the other side of the front and on the front corners of the sides.

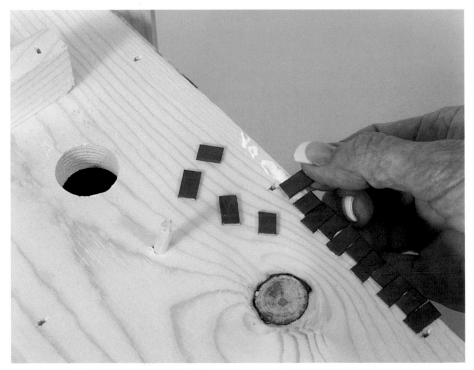

Glue bricks of alternating sizes along the front edge of the house.

Quaint Birdhouses You Can Paint and Decorate

## 4 Trim the Door

Transfer the door pattern to a piece of cardboard, cut it out and basecoat the cutout with Hauser Dark Green. Glue it to the front of the house. Cut ¼-inch long bricks, and glue them around the door.

## 5 Apply the Mortar

Spread the mortar patch on the sides of the house as you would apply plaster to a wall. Use a small painting knife to pat it on, then spread it as evenly as possible. Use the tip of the knife to push the mortar up to the edges of the bricks. Let dry.

## 6 Paint the House

Basecoat the house and awning with Eggshell. Basecoat the roof with Hauser Dark Green. Paint Hauser Dark Green stripes on the awning.

## 7 Paint the Base

Paint the base with a light coat of Red Iron Oxide, then randomly dab with Brandy Wine and Uniform Blue. Sponge lightly over the paint with a small piece of foam to blend and soften colors. Let dry. Use Eggshell on a liner brush to paint the mortar lines.

## 8 Make the Sign

To cut oval ends, use the end of a jumbo craft stick as a pattern to draw a cutting line 2¾-inch from the end of another stick. Use a craft knife or pruning shears to cut the stick. Sand the cut end. Basecoat the sign with Hauser Dark Green. Paint the border and lettering with Glorious Gold.

## 9 Assemble the Window

Illustrated step-by-step instructions are on page 88. Cut a six-square piece of welded wire. Cut 2½-inch shutters from a craft stick. Paint the shutters with Hauser Dark Green. To create the look of inset

Use a small painting knife to spread mortar patch on the house.

panels, use Lamp Black to paint two sides an upside-down L-shape. Highlight the other two sides with Hauser Dark Green + Titanium White. Use the welded wire as a guide to draw the shape of the window with a pencil. Paint the window with Lamp Black. When dry, glue wire over the window and glue shutters on either side.

## 10 Finishing Touches

Use Glorious Gold to paint the kickplate and door pulls on the door. Make the urns by gluing wooden beads together. Paint the urns with Glorious Gold. Fill them with miniature greenery.

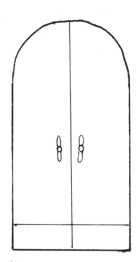

Door and sign pattern.

A plain birdhouse can be changed in many ways with just a few architectural details. This hotel's brick facade is easily designed by a simple trick of sponging over masking tape.

HOTEL

Rooms 50¢

Hot Bath 25¢

WELCOME

# Hotel

Simple wood cutouts add character and interest to the hotel.

## Materials

- tall birdhouse with base
- triangular wood cutout for porch cover
- wood cutout for door: 1½" x 3¼" x ⅛"
- cedar shingles (available where doll-house supplies are sold)
- basswood strips: one ⅛" x ¼", one ¹⁄₁₆" x ¼", one ³⁄₃₂" x ³⁄₃₂"
- craft sticks (regular and jumbo)
- vinyl window screen
- ½"-wide masking tape

### DecoArt Americana acrylic paints
- Rockwood Red
- Burnt Sienna
- Red Iron Oxide
- Driftwood
- Lamp Black
- Burnt Umber
- Milk Chocolate
- Buttermilk
- Neutral Grey
- Khaki Tan

### Apple Barrel acrylic paints
- Midnight Blue

### Brushes
- 1" synthetic flat or 1" sponge
- no. 4, 6 and 8 flats
- no. 0 liner

## 1 Basecoat and Sponge

Sand the birdhouse and porch cover. Wipe with a tack cloth. Squeeze Rockwood Red, Burnt Sienna, Red Iron Oxide and Midnight Blue onto the palette. Cut a 2-inch square of foam. Pull corners up to form a pouf. Dip the pouf into Rockwood Red and sponge the sides of the house. Only minimal coverage is needed since any bare wood can be covered with subsequent colors. Next, dip the sponge into Burnt Sienna and sponge over the base color, allowing the base color to show through. Repeat with Red Iron Oxide. Dip the sponge into Midnight Blue. Blot the sponge on the palette to remove most of the paint. Sponge blue on the house sparingly. If the blue is too heavy or looks spotty in places, dip the sponge into Red Iron Oxide and sponge over those areas. Let dry. Basecoat the roof, porch cover and basswood strips with Driftwood. Use Burnt Umber on the chisel edge of a no. 4 brush to paint shading lines across the porch piece to create the look of board siding. Paint the base of the house Neutral Grey.

## 2 Tape Off Bricks

Use ½-inch wide masking tape to create the lines of mortar between the bricks. Work one side of the house at a time. Starting at the bottom, place one strip of tape across the side of the house. Leave approximately a ¹⁄₁₆-inch space and place another strip above the first one. Repeat until the side of the house is covered.

After basecoat and sponging are dry, apply tape to the house.

## 3 Paint the Mortar Lines

Use a foam pouf to pat the Driftwood over the openings between the strips of tape. Remove the tape.

Use a foam pouf to sponge the unmasked portion of the house.

Quaint Birdhouses You Can Paint and Decorate

## 4 Reapply Tape

When the paint is dry, apply the tape again so that the open lines fall halfway between the first lines. This will create mortar lines in between the first ones. Sponge the open lines with Driftwood. Remove the tape.

Apply the tape again so that the open lines fall halfway between the first lines.

## 5 Paint Vertical Mortar Lines

Use Driftwood on a liner brush to paint the vertical lines of mortar. Remember to alternate lines on each row.

Paint vertical lines of mortar.

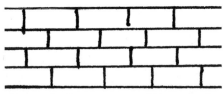

Diagram for alternating vertical lines in brickwork.

# 6 Make the Windows and Door

To make the windows, cut eight 1⅞-inch pieces from jumbo craft sticks. Basecoat the window pieces and door cutout with Khaki Tan. Cut vinyl window screen the same size as the windows and door. Glue screen over each piece. Use a craft knife to cut ³⁄₃₂" x ³⁄₃₂" basswood strips (previously painted) to fit around the window edges. Glue the strips to the windows. Cut ³⁄₃₂" x ³⁄₃₂" strips the same length as the sides of the door. Glue along edges. Cut three strips of ¹⁄₁₆" x ¼" basswood to fit between side pieces. Glue strips at the top, middle and bottom of the door. Glue the windows and door in place.

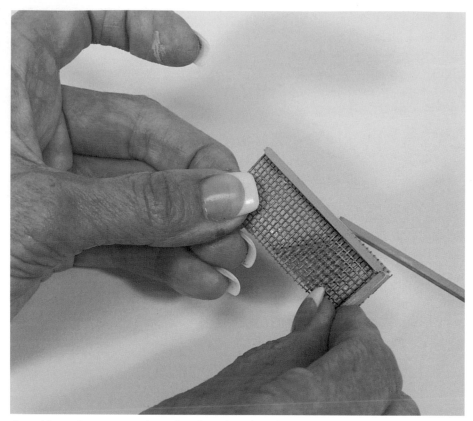

Assemble windows using jumbo craft sticks and vinyl window screen.

Attach the windows.

Quaint Birdhouses You Can Paint and Decorate

## 7 Shingle the Roof

Squeeze a line of glue along the bottom edge of the roof. Press the first row of shingles into place along the glue line, allowing them to overhang the roof slightly but keeping the bottom edges even. Squeeze another line of glue directly onto the top edge of the first row of shingles and a second line onto the roof approximately ½-inch above the shingles. Starting with a narrow shingle, press the second row in place, overlapping the bottom edge of the second row onto the top edge of the first row. Repeat this process until the entire roof is covered, starting alternate rows with narrow shingles. This will vary the pattern of shingles so the shingles are not in even vertical rows. Check spacing of shingles along one edge to be sure the last row ends at the top edge of the roof. If not, adjust the spacing of the rows as you work. Apply shingles to the porch with the same process. Some shingles may need to be broken in half vertically to create variety in spacing.

Glue cedar shingles onto the roof.

## 8 Add the Porch Cover

Position triangular porch cover on front of house. Glue in place. From ⅛" x ¼" basswood, cut two pieces for support posts between the porch cover and base. Glue in place.

## 9 Finishing Touches

**Welcome mat.** To make the welcome mat, cut a 1⅛-inch piece from a jumbo craft stick. Basecoat with Milk Chocolate + Buttermilk. Use a liner brush to letter "Welcome" and to paint a border with Burnt Umber.

**Signs.** To make the "Hotel" sign, cut a 1⅛-inch piece from a jumbo craft stick. Basecoat the sign with Khaki Tan. Use Lamp Black on a liner brush to write letters and paint the border. To make the "rooms" and "bath" signs, cut a 1½-inch long piece from a regular craft stick and a 1½-inch piece from a jumbo craft stick. Basecoat with Buttermilk. Use the photo on page 24 as a guide to do lettering and trim with a black permanent pen. Glue the signs and mat in place with heavy craft glue.

**Note:** When lettering, it's always a good idea to first print the letters lightly with a pencil to check size and spacing. When spacing is right, draw over pencil lines with paint or marker, let dry, then erase pencil lines.

# Church

## Materials

- church-shaped birdhouse
- aquarium rock
- silicone sealant or glue
- wood piece for step: ⅜" x ⅜" x 2"

*DecoArt Americana acrylic paints*
- Titanium White
- Graphite
- Lamp Black
- Dove Grey
- Winter Blue
- Golden Straw
- Yellow Light
- Raw Sienna
- Glorious Gold

*Brushes*
- 1" synthetic flat or 1" sponge
- no. 2 and 6 flats
- no. 0 liner and round detail
- fan brush

*Optional accessories*
- two ¼" candle cups
- miniature flowers

## 1 Basecoat the Church

Paint the church with Titanium White. Paint the base and the step with Dove Grey. Glue the step in place.

## 2 Paint the Roof

Basecoat the roof of the church and the bell tower with Graphite. While the paint is wet, use a fan brush to make short, upward strokes of Dove Grey to indicate rows of shingles. After the rows are established with the light color, shade under each row with Lamp Black.

## 3 Make the Windows

Choose the smallest aquarium rocks for the windows of the church. The design on the windows on the front of the church is random. To get a symmetrical shape for the window, fold a piece of paper in half, then cut a window pattern. Position the cutout on the birdhouse to check the size. If the size is right, lightly draw around the pattern with a pencil. Squeeze a line of silicone sealant or glue along a section of the outline. Press a row of rocks into the glue to form the outline of the window. Keep the edges as straight as possible. Outline the entire window. Next, position and glue the rocks that form the focal point of the design, such as the cross. Fill in the rest of the window.

## 4 Paint the Bell Tower

Use a pencil to draw the outline of the opening on all four sides of the tower. Draw a bell in each opening. Paint the sky with Winter Blue and Winter Blue + Titanium White. Paint the bell with Yellow Light, shaded with Golden Straw and highlighted with Yellow Light + Titanium White. Paint supports with Raw Sienna.

## 5 Final Touches

Draw the outline of the doors with a pencil, then redraw with a black permanent pen. Paint the door plates and candle cups Glorious Gold. Use the handle end of the brush to dot the doorknobs with Glorious Gold. Glue miniature flowers into the candle cups, and glue the candle cups to the base.

After sizing and drawing the window pattern, begin gluing rocks on the window outline.

Form the focal point of the window design, such as this cross.

Fill the entire window.

ontrol four-alarm fires in the village
with this fully equipped fire station.
Easily assembled miniatures, such as the
ladder, axe and water hose, give the
final fire-fighting touch.

Quaint Birdhouses You Can Paint and Decorate

# Fire Station

## 1 Basecoat With a Color Wash

Sand the birdhouse and wipe with a tack cloth. Mix equal parts of Neutral Grey and Multi-Purpose Sealer. Use the mix to basecoat the house with a wash of gray.

Use a mix of Neutral Grey and DecoArt Multi-Purpose Sealer to give the station a gray wash.

| Materials |
| --- |
| • barn-style craft store birdhouse |
| • ⅛" x ¼" basswood strips |
| • craft sticks (regular and jumbo) |
| • ½" x ½" welded wire: two 4-square pieces |
| • DecoArt Multi-Purpose Sealer |
| • drill with ¹⁄₁₆" bit |
| • small nails |
| • 20-gauge wire |
| • wire cutters |

### DecoArt Americana acrylic paints
- Neutral Grey
- Soft Black
- Lamp Black
- Country Red
- White Wash
- Antique Gold
- Tomato Red
- Glorious Gold

### Apple Barrel acrylic paints
- Midnight Blue

### Brushes
- 1" synthetic flat or 1" sponge
- no. 4 and 6 flats
- no. 0 liner

| Optional Accessories |
| --- |
| • ¼" wooden bell |
| • two carpet tacks |
| • wood cutout for sign: 2¾" x ¾" x ⅛" |
| • cording for hose |
| • air-dry or oven-bake clay for nozzle |
| • heavy white string |
| • twig logs |
| • toolbox: 1⅜" x ⅜" x ⅜" with U-nail handle |
| • miniature axe |
| • eye ring |

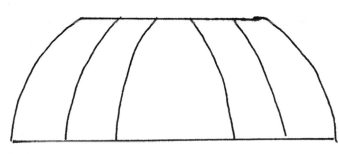

Awning pattern.

## 2 Draw Siding

Use a liner brush with thinned Soft Black to paint vertical lines to suggest board siding.

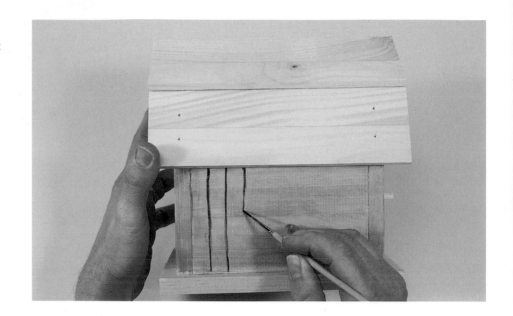

## 3 Add More Color Tints

Overstroke with a very thin wash of Midnight Blue to add color variation and interest to the basecoat.

## 4 Soften and Age the Color

While wet, apply another thin wash of Neutral Grey.

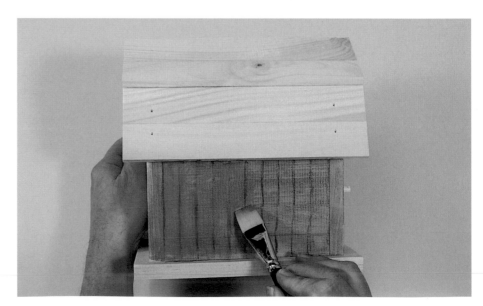

Quaint Birdhouses You Can Paint and Decorate

## 5 Add Trim and Accessories

**Door.** Measure and mark a 2¾" x 4" rectangle for the doors. Paint the doors and roof Country Red. Paint the sign and basswood strips with White Wash. Cut strips to fit around the door; glue in place. Use carpet tacks for door handles.

**Sign.** Letter the sign with a liner brush and thinned Lamp Black. Glue the sign above the door.

**Windows.** Cut two 4-square pieces of welded wire. Paint with Soft Black. Glue on the side of the house.

**Shutters.** Cut 1-inch shutters from craft sticks and paint with White Wash. Glue in place.

**Awnings.** Cut two awnings from jumbo craft sticks. Paint the awnings White Wash and stripes Tomato Red, outlined with Lamp Black. Glue in place.

**Bell.** Paint the bell Antique Gold and the stripes Soft Black.

**Toolbox.** Paint the toolbox Soft Black.

**Fire hose.** Cut a 15-inch length of cording. Shape a nozzle with air-dry or oven-bake clay. Poke a hole in one end to fit the cording. When dry, glue the nozzle to the end of the cording. Paint the nozzle Glorious Gold. Wrap cording into a coil and glue to hold.

**Rope.** Cut a 15-inch length of string. Form it into a coil and glue to hold.

**Final assembly.** Hang the hose, rope and ladder using nails. Spot glue to secure. Screw an eye ring into the top of the bell, then tie a string to the ring and hang it under the roof overhang. Glue the logs, axe and toolbox in place.

## How to Make a Ladder

Cut eight ⅞-inch lengths of 20-gauge wire. Cut two 4⅜-inch basswood strips. Use a drill or small nail to make eight evenly spaced holes in each strip.

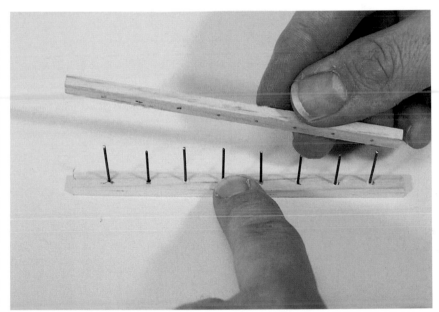

Glue the wire ends into the holes. Paint the ladder with White Wash.

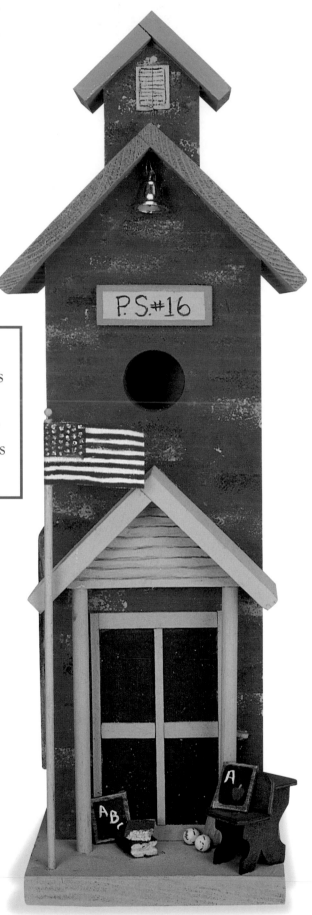

omplete with desk, blackboard
and brass bell, this schoolhouse is
smartly accessorized with craft sticks,
dowels and balsa strips. The brick technique demonstrated here easily transfers
to other projects.

# Schoolhouse

## 1 Basecoat

Sand the birdhouse, bell tower and porch cover well. Wipe with a tack cloth. Basecoat the sides of the house and bell tower with Brandy Wine. Paint the roofs Williamsburg Blue. Paint the base and porch cover with Driftwood.

### Materials

- tall birdhouse
- porch cover with columns
- bell tower
- basswood or balsa strips: $\frac{1}{16}$" x $\frac{1}{4}$", $\frac{3}{32}$" x $\frac{3}{32}$"
- drill with $\frac{1}{16}$" and $\frac{1}{8}$" bits
- fine wire
- wire cutters
- upholstery foam

*DecoArt Americana acrylic paints*
- Brandy Wine
- Driftwood
- Soft Black
- Williamsburg Blue
- Tomato Red
- True Blue
- Titanium White
- Burnt Umber
- Lamp Black
- Metallic Silver

*Brushes*
- 1" synthetic flat or 1" sponge
- no. 2 and 6 flats
- no. 0 liner
- no. 0 round detail

### Optional Accessories

- $\frac{1}{2}$" brass bell
- 1" x 1½" strip of white fabric
- $\frac{1}{8}$" dowel: 7¼" long
- straight pin with bead head
- jumbo craft sticks
- wood cutout for sign: $\frac{5}{8}$" x 2⅛"
- miniature balls and bat
- 2" x 4" craft store blackboard or bristol board
- $\frac{1}{8}$" x ½" balsa strip
- miniature school desk

## 2 Cut the Sponge

To create the used brick on the house and bell tower, cut a ¼" x ⅝" piece of foam to use for sponging.

## 3 Sponge the Brick

Squeeze Brandy Wine, Driftwood and Soft Black onto the palette. Dip the sponge into Driftwood. Pat on the palette to remove excess paint and distribute the paint evenly. Pat the sponge on the house in a hit-or-miss pattern, keeping in mind that bricks must be in straight rows.

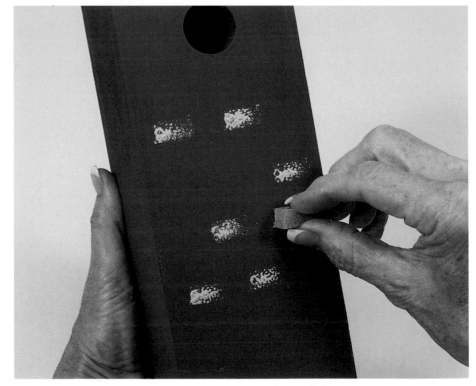

In a hit-or-miss pattern, sponge the first color, Driftwood, onto the house.

Quaint Birdhouses You Can Paint and Decorate

## 4 Sponge Additional Colors

Repeat with Soft Black. Sponge again with Brandy Wine to soften and blend colors and create the appearance of worn, used brick.

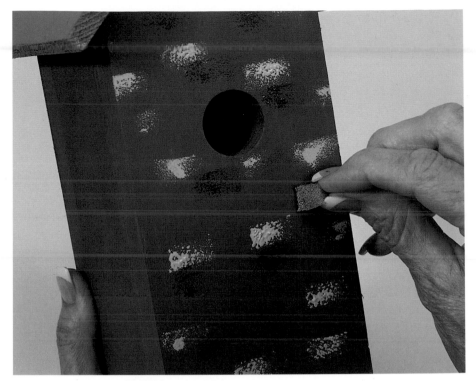

Add the second color, Soft Black.

Finish sponging with Brandy Wine to soften and blend colors.

## 5 Paint the Door and Trim

Use a pencil and ruler to draw a 2" x 3½" rectangle for the door. Paint the door Soft Black. Use a craft knife to cut ¼-inch wide basswood strips to fit the door. Cut a center strip from ³⁄₃₂" x ³⁄₃₂" basswood. Paint the door trim with Driftwood. Let dry, then glue in place. Use the chisel edge of a no. 2 brush to draw boards on the porch cover with Soft Black. Glue the porch cover to the front of the house.

Trim the door.

## 6 Make a Blackboard

Cut a 2" x 4" piece of bristol board or medium-weight cardboard. Basecoat with a mixture of Lamp Black and a touch of Titanium White. Cut the frame strips from basswood. (Strips should fit on top of the blackboard, not around it, so they can be glued more securely.) Stain the strips with Burnt Umber. Glue the strips to the blackboard.

Attach basswood strips to bristol board (or cardboard) to make the blackboard.

Quaint Birdhouses You Can Paint and Decorate

# 7 Finishing Touches

**Bell tower.** To make the vent in the bell tower, cut a ½-inch wide piece from a jumbo craft stick. Basecoat with Driftwood. Draw vent lines with a black permanent pen. Glue the vent to the bell tower. Glue the bell tower to the rooftop.

**School sign.** Basecoat the sign with Driftwood. Paint a border of Williamsburg Blue. Use a black permanent pen to write the school name.

**Flag.** Use a paper flag, or, to make the flag, draw the shape of the flag on white fabric. Paint seven stripes with Tomato Red. Paint the background for the stars with True Blue. Use a toothpick or stylus to make the stars by making dots, then pulling points from the dots. When dry, cut out flag. Cut a 7¼-inch length of a ⅛-inch dowel. Cut the straight pin off ¼-inch below the bead. Insert and glue the bead head in the end of the dowel. Paint the dowel and bead head with Metallic Silver. Glue the flag to the pole. Drill a hole in the base, and glue the flagpole into hole.

**Balls and bat.** If the bat is unfinished, stain it with thinned Burnt Umber. Paint the handgrip with Soft Black. Paint ¼-inch beads or balls with Titanium White. Use a black pen for stitching.

**Slates, blackboard and books.** To make the slates, cut ½-inch pieces from jumbo craft sticks. Stain with thinned Burnt Umber. Paint the center areas with black. Use red to draw an apple and white to write letters. Cut books from ⅛" x ½" balsa strips. Paint the edges with white and the covers with red or green. Use a liner brush with slightly thinned white to letter the blackboard.

**Finish.** Attach the bell to the roof by drilling a small hole in the peak of the roof. Run a fine wire through the top of the bell and glue the wire ends into the hole. Glue blackboard to the side of the school and the sign to the front. Arrange other accessories on the porch, and glue in place.

*T*he depot takes a place of proud distinction in town with this bright, textured roof. The platform provides the perfect spot to leave luggage and other travel items.

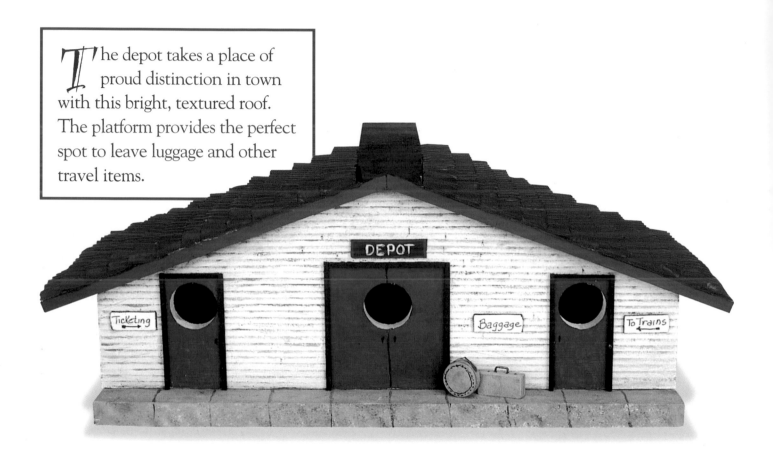

Quaint Birdhouses You Can Paint and Decorate

# Depot

## 1 Make the Tile Roof

One-sided corrugated cardboard, often used in packing, is used to make the tile roof. It is available in some stores where gift wrap or packing supplies are sold. Cut the cardboard into ½- to ⅝-inch wide strips that are long enough to fit across the roof. Beginning at the bottom of the roof, squeeze a line of glue along the bottom edge of the roof. Press the first strip of cardboard into place along the glue line, matching the bottom of the cardboard to the bottom of the roof. Squeeze another line of glue directly onto the top edge of the first strip and a second line on the roof approximately ½-inch above the strip. Press the second strip in place, overlapping the top edge of the first strip. Check spacing of the rows along one edge to be sure the last row ends at the top edge of the roof. Adjust spacing if needed. Let dry.

### Materials

- craft store birdhouse
- one-sided corrugated cardboard
- craft sticks
- ³⁄₃₂" x ³⁄₃₂" basswood strips
- red spray paint
- upholstery foam
- ⅛"-wide masking tape or ruler
- small wood pieces for luggage
- red spray paint

*Acrylic paints*
- black
- white
- dark green
- khaki

*Brushes*
- 1" synthetic flat or 1" sponge
- no. 6 and 8 flats
- no. 0 liner

## How to Make One-Sided Corrugated Cardboard

One-sided corrugated cardboard can be made from an ordinary cardboard box. Cut the box apart, then thoroughly wet the sections of the box. Peel away one side of the plain paper, exposing the ribbed inner piece. After removing one side, set the cardboard aside to dry until you are ready to use it.

## 2 Spray Paint the Roof

Before the rest of the house is painted, spray paint the roof red so that any overspray can be covered with the base color. When dry, touch up any bare spots with red acrylic paint. The color does not need to match exactly; there are color variations in real tiles.

After painting the base with a mixture of black and white, pat the surface with a foam sponge to soften the color and remove excess paint.

## 3 Paint the Base

To create the look of cement, brush mix black and white as you work. This creates color variations. Use the corner of a no. 6 brush to dab paint onto the base. Use enough paint for good coverage. While the paint is wet, pat the surface with the foam sponge to soften the color and remove excess paint. Do not overblend. Use thinned black on a liner brush to draw the cracks into the cement.

## 4 Tape Off Siding

After basecoating the birdhouse white, cover the house with ⅛-inch masking tape (you can find ⅛-inch masking tape at auto supply stores). Start at the bottom of the house and work one side at a time. Leave a very narrow line between strips.

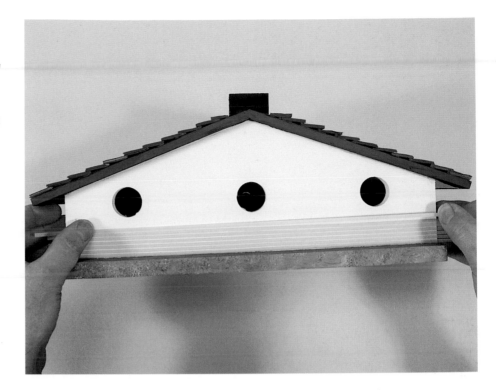

## 5 Paint the Siding

To paint the board siding, use black paint on an old brush or piece of foam to fill in the open spaces between the strips of tape. Remove the tape and repeat the same process on the other three sides. Use thinned black on a liner brush to make a few vertical lines in the boards. Another way to paint board siding is to use a pencil and ruler to draw the rows, then use black on the chisel edge of a dry-wiped brush to paint over the pencil lines.

## 6 Paint the Trim

Use a pencil and ruler to draw the outline of the doors. Paint the doors and eaves of the house dark green. Paint the top piece on the roof black.

## 7 Make Door Molding

To make the door molding, use a craft knife to cut basswood strips into pieces to fit around the doors. Paint the basswood strips black. Glue in place.

Quaint Birdhouses You Can Paint and Decorate

The luggage can be made with a ¾-inch dowel or ½-inch piece of wood, then painted and detailed with paper handles.

## 8 Paint Signs

Use a craft knife or shears to cut signs from craft sticks. Basecoat the "Depot" sign with black. Use white on a liner brush to letter the sign. Paint the other signs white with black edges. Letter the signs with a black permanent pen. Glue signs to the birdhouse.

## 9 Make the Luggage

Cut the luggage from a ¾-inch dowel or ½-inch wood. Sponge with a khaki color. Use a pen to add detail. Make handles from brown paper or a small staple or U-nail. Glue the luggage on the platform.

Try adapting your own quilt design to coordinate this cheerful shop to whatever's in your home. Small sewing items, such as buttons or lace, make creative additions.

The Quilting Bee

BUSY IS A BEE

OPEN 9-5

# Quilt Shop

## 1 Basecoat and Sponge

Sand the house well and wipe with a tack cloth. Basecoat the house with Williamsburg Blue. Spatter with slightly thinned Wedgewood Blue. Paint the roof and base Ice Blue.

### Materials

- craft store birdhouse
- four small buttons
- jumbo craft stick

*Delta Ceramcoat acrylic paints*
- White
- Ivory
- Bright Red
- Black Cherry
- Coral
- Burnt Sienna
- Raw Sienna
- Black
- Wedgewood Blue
- Empire Gold
- Spice Brown

*DecoArt Americana acrylic paints*
- Ice Blue
- Uniform Blue
- Williamsburg Blue
- Hauser Medium Green

*Folk Art acrylic paint*
- Bluegrass

*Brushes*
- 1" synthetic flat or 1" sponge
- no. 2, 6 and 8 flats
- no. 0 liner
- no. 0 round detail
- stiff bristle or old toothbrush

## 2 Paint the Roof Design

Transfer the quilt outline to the roof. Basecoat the center with Ivory and the border with Black Cherry. Paint a 5-square cross of Williamsburg Blue.

Shade the Ivory squares with Burnt Sienna and the blue squares with Uniform Blue.

Use a liner brush to crosshatch the Ivory squares with Bright Red. Use Wedgewood Blue to paint the plaid design on the blue squares. Paint a heart on each blue square with Black Cherry. Use Ivory for the stitches on the border.

To paint the yo-yos, divide a scalloped circle into sections. Paint each section a different color. Outline with a black pen.

Add dots and linework.

Basecoat the bee with Empire Gold shaded with Raw Sienna. Paint the wings White. Dot the head Black.

Outline the wings and add feelers and feet with a black pen. Draw the black stripes on the body.

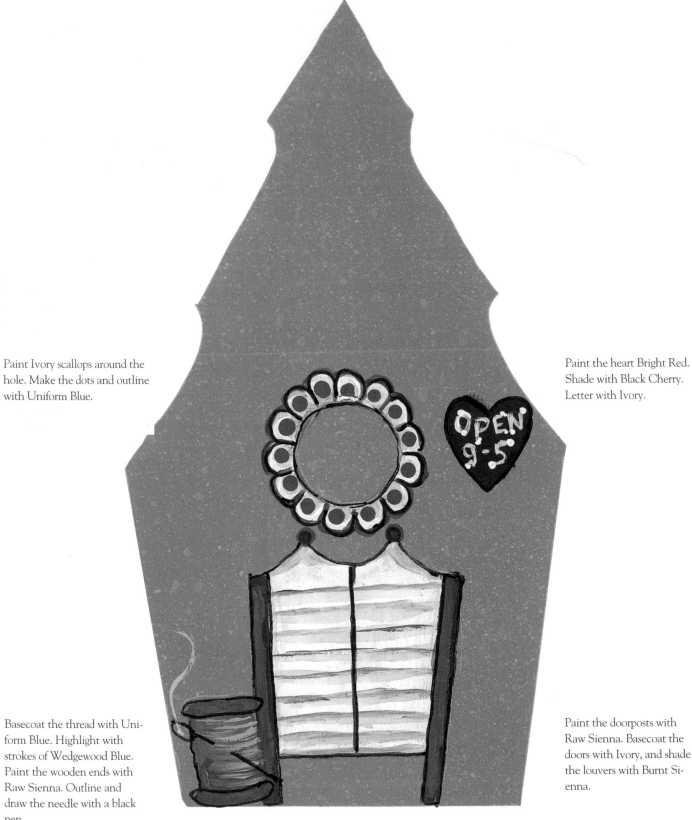

Paint Ivory scallops around the hole. Make the dots and outline with Uniform Blue.

Paint the heart Bright Red. Shade with Black Cherry. Letter with Ivory.

Basecoat the thread with Uniform Blue. Highlight with strokes of Wedgewood Blue. Paint the wooden ends with Raw Sienna. Outline and draw the needle with a black pen.

Paint the doorposts with Raw Sienna. Basecoat the doors with Ivory, and shade the louvers with Burnt Sienna.

# 4 Paint the Side Windows

Basecoat the curtains Ivory and the rest of the window Coral + White. Make squiggle flowers with Bright Red, highlighted with Ivory. Paint the shutters Black Cherry. Basecoat sewing machine Black.

Paint the window trim with Burnt Sienna. Highlight the sewing machine with White. Use Bright Red for the thread spool. Shade around the windows with Burnt Sienna.

Use Bluegrass for the linework on the curtains. Paint the leaves on the wallpaper with Hauser Medium Green. Paint the shutter louvers Ivory.

Paint the fabric bolts with Bright Red, Bluegrass and Empire Gold. Make White polka dots on the red fabric and black cross-hatching on the gold fabric.

## 5 Shade the Roof
Shade the edges of the roof and the base with Spice Brown.

## 6 Make the Sign
To cut the oval ends, use the end of a jumbo craft stick as a pattern to draw a cutting line 2¾-inch from the end of another stick. Use a craft knife or pruning shears to cut the stick. Sand cut the end. Basecoat the sign with Ivory. Write letters and outline the bumblebee with a black permanent pen. Paint the bumblebee with Empire Gold with White wings and Black stripes.

*M*ake this house as a charming accent piece for the kitchen. The idea can be adapted to any size birdhouse. Cinnamon sticks are available in a variety of lengths at craft stores and kitchen shops. They can also be easily cut with a jigsaw or band saw.

All Spice

# Spice Shop

## 1 Preparation

Sand the birdhouse well. Wipe with a tack cloth to remove dust particles. Cut out a sign from a jumbo craft stick, and cut the gingerbread boys from medium-weight cardboard.

## 2 Basecoat

Basecoat the sign with Williamsburg Blue. Basecoat the house and base with Antique White. Paint the roof with Raw Sienna and the flat piece at the top of the roof with Red Iron Oxide.

## 3 Paint the Checkerboard Squares

With Williamsburg Blue on a no. 10 brush, paint checkerboard bricks beginning at the base and working up the front and sides. Make the bricks darker and more distinct near the corners of the house, gradually making them lighter and more random as you work toward the middle.

### Materials

- craft store birdhouse
- cinnamon sticks: about thirty 3", two 4½"
- jumbo craft stick
- ⅛"-wide masking tape
- small wooden or cinnamon hearts (½")
- gingerbread boy cutouts or medium-weight cardboard (not corrugated)
- fabric scraps for curtains
- toothpick

*DecoArt Americana acrylic paints*
- Eggshell
- Antique White
- Honey Brown
- Williamsburg Blue
- Light Cinnamon
- Burnt Umber
- Avocado
- Moon Yellow
- DeLane's Cheek Color
- Tomato Red
- Red Iron Oxide
- Raw Sienna
- Lamp Black
- Light Buttermilk
- Medium Flesh
- Titanium White

*Brushes*
- 1" synthetic flat or 1" sponge
- no. 2, 6 and 10 flats
- no. 0 liner
- no. 0 round detail
- stiff bristle or old toothbrush

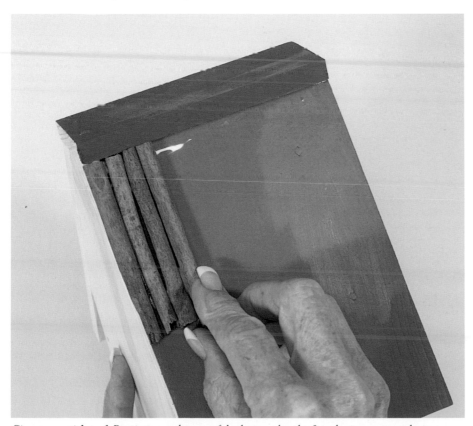

***Cinnamon stick roof.*** Beginning at the top of the house, glue the 3-inch cinnamon sticks in a vertical row across the roof. Glue one long cinnamon stick horizontally at the bottom of the row. Glue another row of 3-inch sticks under the horizontal one to finish covering the roof. Glue the small wooden or cinnamon hearts in a row along the front eaves of the house.

## 4 Paint the Door and Windows

The door and windows on the sample project were drawn freehand with a liner brush. If you prefer using a pattern, sketch the door and windows lightly with a pencil. Basecoat the door with Williamsburg Blue. Underpaint sketchy squares for the windows in the door with Light Buttermilk. Let dry. Paint all of the window panes with a stroke of Moon Yellow. Use thinned Light Cinnamon on a liner brush to paint very loose outlines for the windows and door and to make hash marks on the front and sides of the house.

## 5 Paint the Tree

To paint the tree trunk and larger branches, use Burnt Umber thinned with a little water on a no. 6 brush. Create light and dark values by thinning the paint with more water and using the chisel edge of the brush to stretch the paint, using up-and-down strokes. Strengthen dark values by applying unthinned paint. To paint the foliage, thin Avocado with water and use a patting and sliding motion with the corner of the no. 10 brush to suggest leaves. Leave open spaces for a light, airy tree. Use less water to make darker leaves and define the final shape of the tree.

After sketching the door and windows in pencil, basecoat the door with Williamsburg Blue. Underpaint the windows in the door with Light Buttermilk. Paint the windows in the door and all of the other windows with Moon Yellow.

Use Burnt Umber thinned with water to paint the tree trunk and larger branches. Use Avocado with water to paint the foliage. Suggest leaves by using a patting and sliding motion with the corner of the brush.

Quaint Birdhouses You Can Paint and Decorate

## 6 Paint Grass and Flowers

Use the liner brush and thinned Avocado to pull up grass strokes from the base of the house. To make dot flowers, dip the handle of your brush in DeLane's Cheek Color and press it on the house to make a circle of small dots. Make a dot of Moon Yellow for the centers.

## 7 Paint the Sidewalk Brick

Use ⅛-inch masking tape to mask off mortar lines to make the brick shapes on the base. Sponge the base with Red Iron Oxide. Remove tape immediately.

## 8 Paint the Sign

Draw the lettering on the sign with a pencil to check spacing. Use Antique White on a liner brush to paint over the pencil lines. Draw the heart with Tomato Red. Make a dot flower with Tomato Red with a Moon Yellow center. Paint a border around the sign with Lamp Black.

## 9 Paint the Gingerbread Boys

Basecoat with Honey Brown. Use a toothpick to dot the eyes with Lamp Black. Use a stylus to dot the cheeks with Medium Flesh. Paint the hearts with Tomato Red. Use Titanium White on a liner brush to paint the frosting lines.

## 10 Spattering

To spatter the house, dip a stiff bristle brush into thinned Lamp Black. Hold the brush 6 to 8 inches from the surface and drag a painting knife across the bristles toward you. Let dry.

## 11 Add Curtains and Trim

Cut two 1" x 4" pieces of fabric. Squeeze a line of heavy craft glue about ½-inch above each window. Press fabric over the glue line, gathering the fabric as you work. Glue the gingerbread men to the front of the house.

Pull up grass strokes using a liner brush and thinned Avocado. Dip the handle of your brush in DeLane's Cheek Color to make dot flowers; use Moon Yellow for the centers.

After basecoating with Honey Brown, embellish with dot eyes, rosy cheeks and frosting lines.

T his sweet treat store didn't originally have a shelf; you can build one to fit your house using jumbo craft sticks. The "stone" base for this project is a useful technique for any type of cottage.

# Honey Shop

## 1 Preparation

To make the shelf on the front of the house, cut two jumbo craft sticks to fit between the eaves of the house as shown. Glue them together. To make the sign, cut a ⅝" x 2" rectangle of ⅛-inch thick wood. Paint the shelf and sign as you paint the house, then glue the shelf in place. Sand the birdhouse well and wipe with a tack cloth.

## 2 Basecoat and Sponge

Basecoat the sides of the house, the shelf and the sign with Honey Brown. After it is dry, squeeze Sand and Khaki Tan onto the palette. Wet a sea sponge. Squeeze it as dry as possible. Dip the sponge into Sand, pat it on the palette to remove excess paint, then sponge paint onto the birdhouse. Refill the sponge as needed. Dip the sponge in Khaki Tan and apply sparingly to the house.

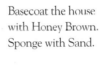

Basecoat the house with Honey Brown. Sponge with Sand.

Sponge very lightly with Khaki Tan.

### Materials

- craft store birdhouse
- jumbo craft sticks
- birch plywood: ⅛" x ⅝" x 2"
- sea sponge
- drill with 1/16" bit
- 20-gauge wire
- wire cutters

*DecoArt Americana acrylic paints*
- Deep Burgundy
- Honey Brown
- Sand
- Khaki Tan
- Burnt Umber
- Raw Sienna
- Yellow Ochre
- Ice Blue
- Titanium White
- Black Plum
- Terra Cotta
- Medium Flesh
- Lavender
- Lilac
- Cadmium Yellow
- Yellow Light
- Avocado
- Summer Lilac
- Blue Violet
- Desert Turquoise

*Brushes*
- 1" synthetic flat or 1" sponge
- no. 2, 4 and 6 flats
- no. 0 liner
- no. 0 round detail
- fan brush

## 3 Paint Shingles

If desired, draw shingle rows lightly with a pencil to check spacing. Use a liner brush to make squiggly rows of shingles with thinned Burnt Umber and Raw Sienna.

## 4 Shade the Roof

To shade under each row, use a fan brush to pull Khaki Tan from the top, then repeat randomly with Raw Sienna.

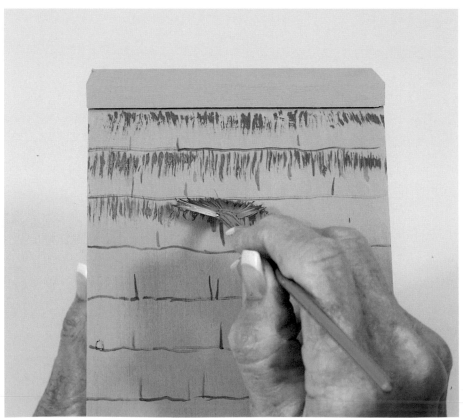

Quaint Birdhouses You Can Paint and Decorate

## 5 Highlight the roof

Highlight each row by pulling Sand upward from the bottom of the shingles.

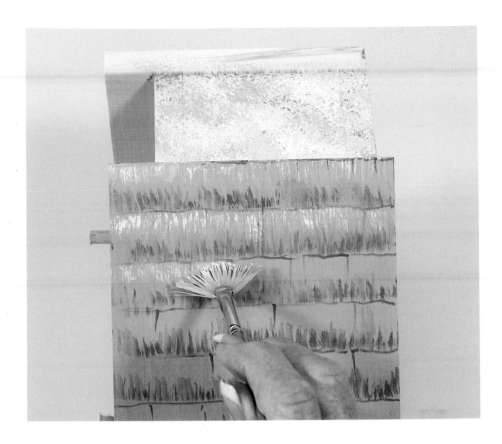

## 6 Paint the Windows

Paint the windows with Ice Blue. Paint the tieback curtain shapes with Titanium White. Outline windows with Black Plum.

# 7 Paint the House Front

**Door.** Paint the door with a wash of Deep Burgundy. Outline with Black Plum.

**Flower pots and beehives.** Sketch the outline of the flowerpots and beehives above the shelf with a pencil. Paint the flowerpots with Terra Cotta. Shade under the rims and along the bottoms with Burnt Umber. Highlight with Medium Flesh. Use a dabbing motion with the corner of a small brush to paint foliage with Avocado and the flowers with Deep Burgundy, Lavender and Lilac. Paint the beehives with Cadmium Yellow. Shade each section and the sides with Raw Sienna. Highlight with Yellow Light. Use thinned Burnt Umber on a liner brush to outline the sections and sides of hives. Draw the holes with Burnt Umber.

**Grass and flowers.** Paint the grass and foliage with thinned Avocado. Use less water and more paint for darker leaves. Paint the flowers by establishing the shape with a middle value, then adding the dark and light values. Use any colors you like, but use three values of each color. The flowers on the sample project are purple: Lavender, Summer Lilac and Lilac; blue: Blue Violet, Desert Turquoise and Desert Turquoise + White; yellow: Cadmium Yellow, Yellow Light and Yellow Light + White. The centers are Raw Sienna + Burnt Umber.

**Wreath.** Establish the shape of the wreath on the door with Burnt Umber linework, then add the leaves, flowers and bow with a small round detail brush, using the same colors as above.

Quaint Birdhouses You Can Paint and Decorate

## 8 Paint the Stone Base

Paint the base of the birdhouse with Sand. Use a no. 6 brush with Khaki Tan, Yellow Ochre and Burnt Umber to make stones. Dip the brush randomly into all three colors, then dab paint onto the surface without blending to create irregular stone shapes. Leave the basecoat showing around the stones for the mortar lines. Varying the pressure on the brush creates color variations in the stones.

## 9 Make the Sign

Drill holes in the sign for the wire. Sponge the edges of the sign with Deep Burgundy. Use a black permanent pen for the lettering. Thread the wire through the holes and hang the sign from a small nail at the peak of the roof. Glue the sign to the eaves to hold it secure.

After basecoating the base with Sand, use several different colors, dabbed randomly, to create irregular stone shapes. Make sure you leave "mortar" lines by leaving space between the stones.

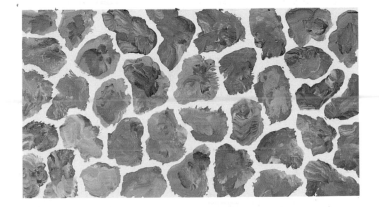

A long piece of upholstery foam efficiently creates shingle rows on this roof. Optional accessories, such as a miniature sewing machine, hatbox and fabric scraps, make this a one-stop shop for every bird's wardrobe (and nest-making) needs!

# Seamstress

## Materials

- birdhouse with porch
- jumbo craft sticks
- upholstery foam

*DecoArt Americana acrylic paints*
- Light Buttermilk
- White Wash
- Blue Mist
- Colonial Green
- Ice Blue
- Green Mist
- Antique Teal
- Coral Rose
- Avocado
- Raw Sienna
- Metallic Silver
- Titanium White

*Brushes*
- 1" synthetic flat or 1" sponge
- no. 6 round
- no. 6 and 10 flats
- no. 0 liner
- no. 0 round detail

## Optional Accessories

- two porch posts (available where doll house supplies are sold)
- welcome mat: 1" x 1⅜" x 1" wood cutout
- sign: ⅜" x 2" x ⅛"
- flat toothpick
- ready-made miniatures: 1" basket and small flowers, sewing machine, bench, pattern
- shirt-weight cardboard
- fabric scraps
- hatbox: cut ⅜" from ⅛" dowel
- ⅛"-wide coral ribbon

### 1 Basecoat the House

Sand the birdhouse well. Wipe with a tack cloth. Basecoat the sides of the house with White Wash. Paint the roof and the base with Blue Mist. Draw the door shape and paint it Colonial Green.

### 2 Double Load the Foam

Cut a ⅝" x 2" strip of upholstery foam. Squeeze Ice Blue and Colonial Green onto the palette. Double-load the sponge by dipping one edge into Ice Blue and the opposite edge into Colonial Green.

### 3 Make Shingle Rows on Roof With Foam

Pat the sponge lightly on the palette to remove excess paint. Pat the rows of shingles, reloading the sponge as needed.

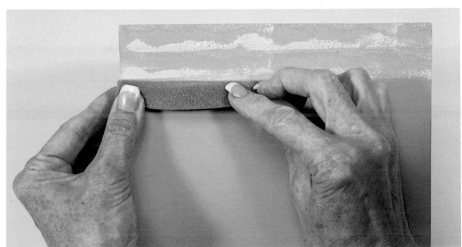

# 4 Outline Shingles

Use a liner brush to loosely outline the rows and define a few shingles with thinned Antique Teal.

# 5 Paint the Flowers

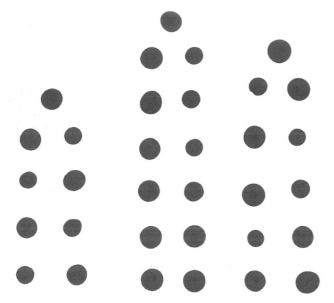

Use the handle end of a large brush to dot the flower with Coral Rose.

Add side petals with strokes of Coral Rose + Titanium White. Add "filler" flowers as shown and add stems.

Make squiggly iris-like flowers with Coral Rose.

Use a liner brush to paint stems and leaves with thinned Avocado + Green Mist.

## 6 Paint the Windows and Shutters

Draw the window shapes lightly with a pencil. Paint the window panes with Ice Blue and the outline trim with Colonial Green. Paint the tieback curtains in the side windows with Blue Mist. Paint the shades in the front windows with Blue Mist, trimmed with Colonial Green. Use Antique Teal to letter the window signs. Cut shutters from jumbo craft sticks to fit the side windows. Paint the shutters Colonial Green. Paint the rectangular shapes with Antique Teal to suggest inset panels.

## 7 Add Optional Accessories

**Porch posts.** Depending on the size of your birdhouse, you may be able to buy pre-made "porch posts" and easily attach them between the base and eaves. The posts for this house measured ⅜-inch.

**Welcome mat.** Paint the welcome mat with Raw Sienna. Use Antique Teal for the border and lettering.

**Hatbox.** Basecoat the hatbox with Light Buttermilk with a Colonial Green lid. Use a detail brush to paint a Coral Rose heart. Do the strokework with Antique Teal. Tie a ⅛"-inch wide coral ribbon around the box.

**Bench.** Paint the bench Colonial Green.

**Fabric.** To make the bolts of fabric, cut ¾" x 1¾" rectangles from light-weight cardboard. Wrap the cardboard with fabric.

**Sign.** Paint the sign with Light Buttermilk. Sponge the edges with Colonial Green, then Antique Teal. Write the letters with a black permanent pen.

**Needle.** To make the needle, paint a toothpick with Metallic Silver and draw the eye with a permanent pen.

**Final assembly.** Glue accessories onto the porch. Glue a miniature sewing machine onto the bench. Glue the sign and toothpick to the front of the house. Paint the basket Titanium White and fill it with miniature flowers. Glue it to the front door.

$\mathcal{A}$ birdhouse with a porch makes a wonderful antique shop and a charming place for displaying small antique-like miniatures. For added interest, use twig branches to replace the porch posts and add a chimney. Complete the picture with a crackled finish to give the birdhouse a time-worn, weathered look.

Quaint Birdhouses You Can Paint and Decorate

# Antique Shop

## 1 Preparation

Cut two 1½-inch pieces from craft sticks, angling ends slightly to look like window boxes. Cut small signs from craft sticks. You may choose to replace the porch posts with twigs and use a larger branch for a chimney.

## 2 Basecoat and Crackle

Paint the sides of the house with Black Green. When dry, trace on the windows and door. Follow the manufacturer's directions to paint the sides of the birdhouse with a heavy but even coat of crackle medium, leaving windows and door unpainted. (See Haunted House for hints on using crackle medium.) Allow to dry as recommended. Paint Shale Green over the crackle medium. Avoid repainting areas because it may lift or smear the color. Allow to dry and crackle. Use a dry-wiped brush to add light vertical streaks of Eggshell over the Shale Green.

Paint the window areas with Eggshell. Paint the door Lamp Black. Use Raspberry to paint the window boxes and the trim around the windows and door. Paint the base of the house Driftwood and the roof Evergreen.

## 3 Add Window Boxes

Glue the window boxes to the house. Use the corner of a small brush to dab foliage in the window boxes with Evergreen and Hauser Light Green. Use the same technique to paint the flowers with Raspberry and Shading Flesh.

## 4 Paint the Signs

Basecoat the small signs with Eggshell. Use Evergreen on a liner brush for lettering. For the large sign, paint a jumbo craft stick with Evergreen. Paint the border and lettering with Shale Green.

## 5 Finishing Touches

Decorate the windows by painting small antiques. Try drawing some of your own special things for a more personalized house. Use a permanent pen for detail and outlining. Glue antique like miniatures on the porch, and glue the signs to the post and roof.

### Materials

- birdhouse with porch
- twig branches for posts and chimney
- craft sticks
- DecoArt Weathered Wood Crackle Medium
- glue gun

*DecoArt Americana acrylic paints*
- Evergreen
- Black Green
- Shale Green
- Eggshell
- Lamp Black
- Shading Flesh
- Driftwood
- Raspberry
- Hauser Light Green

*Brushes*
- 1" synthetic flat or 1" sponge
- no. 2, 6 and 8 flats
- no. 0 liner
- no. 0 round detail

### Optional Accessories

- miniature barrel
- butter churn
- trunk
- bench
- pots and pans
- buckets

For this birdhouse, the antiques are painted with Salem Blue, Burnt Umber and Titanium White.

These houses were done to show how the basic colors and design components for painting one birdhouse can be used on birdhouses of totally different shapes and sizes. The small birdhouse was purchased at the craft store, and nothing was done to enhance it. The tall house had an awning, window and shutters added. Instructions are for the tall house, but the patterns are for both.

# Tea Room

## Materials

- any birdhouse
- ½" x 1" welded wire: two 4-square pieces
- jumbo craft sticks
- awning with braces: 3½" x 2¼" x ¼"
- sea sponge
- wire cutters

### DecoArt Americana acrylic paints
- Moon Yellow
- Shading Flesh
- Graphite
- Colonial Green
- White Wash
- Burnt Umber
- Ice Blue
- Avocado
- Hauser Dark Green
- Raw Sienna
- Deep Burgundy
- Antique Teal
- Victorian Blue
- Antique Gold

### DecoArt Heavenly Hues
- Golden Halo
- White Cloud

### Brushes
- 1" synthetic flat or 1" sponge
- no. 2, 6 and 8 flats
- no. 0 liner
- no. 0 round detail

## 1 Preparation

Cut two 4-square window frames from welded wire. Cut four 2⅛-inch pieces from jumbo craft sticks for the shutters.

## 2 Basecoat

Sand the birdhouse well and wipe with a tack cloth. Basecoat the sides of the house with Moon Yellow. When dry, overstroke with a wash of Golden Halo. Basecoat the roof with Graphite. Use a no. 8 brush to make the checkerboard design on the eaves with Moon Yellow. Stain the base with a wash of Burnt Umber, then draw lines for the boards with unthinned Burnt Umber. Drybrush over the lines to soften them. Paint the awning with Shading Flesh. When dry, overstroke with a wash of White Cloud. Paint the shutters Colonial Green.

## 3 Paint the Windows and Door

Use a pencil to lightly draw the outline of the window. Paint the front window with Golden Halo. Paint café-style curtains with White Wash. Paint the side windows with Ice Blue. While wet, paint tieback curtains in each side window with White Wash. Paint the door with thinned Burnt Umber. Paint the trim around the windows and door with Colonial Green.

Tall house side view.

## 4 Paint the Details

The designs are all painted with slightly thinned paint to achieve a soft, watercolor look. The color used could be changed to fit your personal taste or decor. The designs are simple, so freehanding them, rather than tracing them, will give a softer, less set look to the house.

**Beehive.** Draw the outline of the beehive very lightly with a pencil. Underpaint the beehive with Raw Sienna and shade with Burnt Umber. Highlight with White Wash.

**Bees.** Paint the bees with Antique Gold with White Wash wings.

**Hats and hatrack.** Draw the outline of the hats very lightly with a pencil. Use a wash of Raw Sienna to paint the hats. Overstroke with Antique Gold + White Wash. Paint the ribbons with Deep Burgundy, Antique Teal and Hauser Dark Green, highlighted with White Wash. Basecoat the hatrack Avocado, then shade with Hauser Dark Green.

**Shelves.** Draw the outline of the shelves very lightly with a pencil. Paint the shelf under the front window Burnt Umber. Basecoat the shelf on the sides of the house Avocado, then shade with Hauser Dark Green.

**Signs.** Paint the signs Colonial Green.

**Teapots.** Paint the teapots with Colonial Green.

Quaint Birdhouses You Can Paint and Decorate

## 5 Finish Awning and Windows

Use a liner brush to make the stroke-work design on the shutters with Antique Teal. Paint the trim and lettering on the awning with Colonial Green. When dry, add shadow lines around the letters with a black permanent pen. Glue the welded wire pieces over the side windows with shutters on each side. Glue the awning to the front of the house.

## 6 Paint the Flowers and Vines

**Foliage.** Use a sea sponge or worn-out paintbrush to make the foliage. Paint the foliage with Hauser Dark Green and Hauser Dark Green + Moon Yellow.

**Flowers.** Paint the flowers with the corner of a no. 6 brush, using Deep Burgundy, Victorian Blue and Antique Gold. Lighten colors with White Wash for variety.

**Trellis.** Paint the trellis with Hauser Dark Green.

**Wreath.** Use a liner brush with thinned Burnt Umber to establish the vine stems of the wreath on the front of the house.

Add a Deep Burgundy ribbon. Use a black pen to outline details where needed. Feel free to add personal touches, such as jars of honey, flowerpots or other things that interest you.

## 7 Outline and Letter the Signs

Write lettering on the signs and outline the boards and teapots with a fine black permanent marker.

# Gallery

**Post Office**

Look what can be done by adding magnets to a plain birdhouse. Magnets are available for almost any business or hobby and are ideal for decorating a special interest birdhouse. Created by Richard and Evelyn Rodgers.

## Gas Station

Here's a place where the birds will want to re-fuel and maybe even rest for a spell. Wood cutouts and a tin roof make this country "fill-ing station" suitable for outdoor use. Simple painting adds an inviting, old-time feeling that inspires memories of "quieter, gentler" times.

## General Store

Bring back memories of a quaint little town in rural America with this general store. You can almost hear the screen door bang as you look at the supplies gathered on the porch. Use miniature barrels, a butter churn and crates filled with small wooden balls, painted to look like fruits and vegetables, to add more charm to a finished birdhouse. Add a few minia-ture wooden jars, painted like they are filled with canned goods, and the store is ready to open for business.

A cloth awning is easy to make and creates a comfortable repose from the late summer sun. Brightly colored miniature fruits and vegetables enhance the laid-back air of the market season.

# Farmer's Market

## 1 Basecoat and Paint Bricks

Sand birdhouse and wipe with a tack cloth. Basecoat the house with Driftwood. To paint the look of old bricks or cement blocks, cut a ¼" x ⅝" piece of foam to use for sponging. Squeeze Khaki Tan and Neutral Grey onto the palette. Pat the sponge into Khaki Tan, and then pat it on the palette several times to remove excess paint and to distribute the paint evenly. Pat the paint on the birdhouse in a hit-or-miss pattern. Repeat with Neutral Grey. Basecoat the roof, the porch cover and a 2-inch piece of angle strip with a mix of Antique Teal + Neutral Grey.  Overstroke with a mix of thinned Driftwood + Ice Blue. Paint the base of the house with Khaki Tan + Raw Sienna.

Use thinned Burnt Umber to draw lines to create the boards of a plank floor. To paint the brick chimney, basecoat the chimney with Brandy Wine, then sponge lightly with Rockwood Red. When dry, use a black permanent pen to draw mortar lines. Paint the top of the chimney with Driftwood.

## 2 Make the Windows

Cut eight 1¼-inch long pieces from jumbo craft sticks. Basecoat the sticks with Lamp Black. Let dry, then overstroke them diagonally with Neutral Grey. Paint the window frames and the wood cutout for the door with Brandy Wine. Use Rockwood Red shading to draw panels on the door. When dry, glue the porch cover and angle strip support, the windows and door to the house.

## 3 Paint the Sign on the Roof

To check spacing, use a pencil to lightly draw the lettering for the sign on the roof. Use a no. 2 brush to paint over the pencil line with Driftwood.

### Materials

- birdhouse with a wide base (use any craft store birdhouse and add a wider base)
- fabric for awning
- wood cutout for porch cover: ¼" x 1¼" x 2"
- ½" balsa wood angle strip
- wood cutout for door: ⅛" x 1⅞" x 2½"
- ⅛" wooden dowel
- jumbo craft sticks
- water based satin varnish
- drill with ⅛" bit
- upholstery foam

*DecoArt Americana acrylic paints*
- Driftwood
- Khaki Tan
- Neutral Grey
- Lamp Black
- Brandy Wine
- Rockwood Red
- Antique Teal
- Ice Blue
- Raw Sienna
- Burnt Umber

*Brushes*
- 1" synthetic flat or 1" sponge
- no. 2, 6 and 8 flats
- no. 0 liner
- no. 0 round detail

In this close-up you can see how the random sponging pattern imitates the look of old cement brick. The windows were cut from jumbo craft sticks, basecoated with Lamp Black and overstroked with Neutral Grey.

To make an awning, measure the area to be covered. Double the measurement from the house to the edge of the base, then add 2 inches and cut fabric to size. Paint the back side of the fabric with satin varnish. Fold the fabric in half crosswise. Press layers together with your fingers. When dry, fold down ½-inch along the folded edge and ½-inch on the opposite edge. The folded edge will be the front of the awning. Measure the length needed for the support poles (about 3 inches) and cut dowels to size. Drill holes for poles. Insert and glue the dowels into the holes. Glue the back edge of the awning to the house and the front edge over the poles.

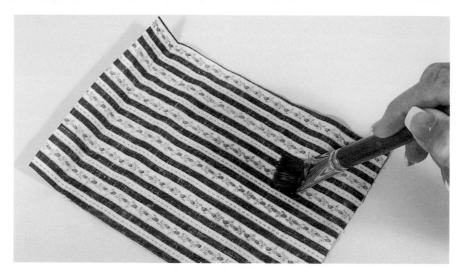

Coat the back side of the fabric with satin varnish.

Fold the fabric in half crosswise and press the layers together.

After cutting the dowels to the correct size, glue the back edge of the awning to the house and the front edge over the poles.

## 4 Finishing Touches

To finish the market, use purchased miniatures. Fill barrels and buckets with small balls painted with red for apples or orange for oranges. Add miniature pumpkins and squash, available in craft stores. Make carrots and potatoes from clay. Make corn shuck bundles from tamale wrappers. Scatter small fall-colored leaves on the floor. Use craft glue or silicone sealant to attach accessories.

### Optional Accessories

- assorted miniatures: baskets, barrels, buckets, wheelbarrows and vegetables
- cornhusk tamale wrappers
- fall leaves
- oven-bake or air-dry clay: orange and brown
- fabric for feed sack
- small wooden balls

$W$ith the natural look so popular, a birdhouse enhanced with bits and pieces of things found growing wild in nature is a perfect decorating accessory. The roof can be covered with bark from a birch tree, or you can paint a birchlike look on a brown bag or wrapping paper. Add final touches with chairs made from mushrooms and twigs, tiny bunches of flowers and rustic signs.

Quaint Birdhouses You Can Paint and Decorate

# Herb Shop

### Materials

- birdhouse with porch
- twig branches for chimney and posts
- craft sticks for signs
- heavy brown paper
- small nails

*DecoArt Americana acrylic paints*
- Sand
- Milk Chocolate
- Burnt Sienna

*Brushes*
- 1" synthetic flat or 1" sponge
- no. 0 liner

### Optional Accessories

- green moss
- dried flowers and herbs
- heavy thread
- bits of bark wood and dried mushrooms
- interesting bits from potpourri mixes

## 1 Replace Porch Posts

To create a rustic look, replace porch posts with twigs and add a chimney with twig branches.

## 2 Make the Roof

To make the birchlike paper for the roof, cut heavy brown paper 1-inch larger all around than the roof measurement. Brush mix a touch of Milk Chocolate into Sand and basecoat the paper. Brush mixing creates a color variation in the basecoat.

Basecoat the "birch" roof with Milk Chocolate and Sand.

## 3 Add Roof Details

Use Burnt Sienna + Milk Chocolate on a liner brush to paint straight strokes of varying lengths across the paper. Let dry.

## 4 Trim and Attach Roof

Trim the paper to fit the roof, snipping the front and back edges in an irregular jagged pattern. Spread craft glue over the roof and press paper smoothly over the glue. Add bits of bark or other materials to enhance the look of peeling bark.

Use a liner brush to add roof details.

## 5 Embellish

Decorate the birdhouse with items such as various kinds of moss, dried flowers, mushrooms and potpourri bits. Tie dried flowers into small bunches. Make chairs from slices of wood and dried mushrooms. Cut and stain craft sticks for signs. Use small nails and glue to attach trimmings.

Herb Shop

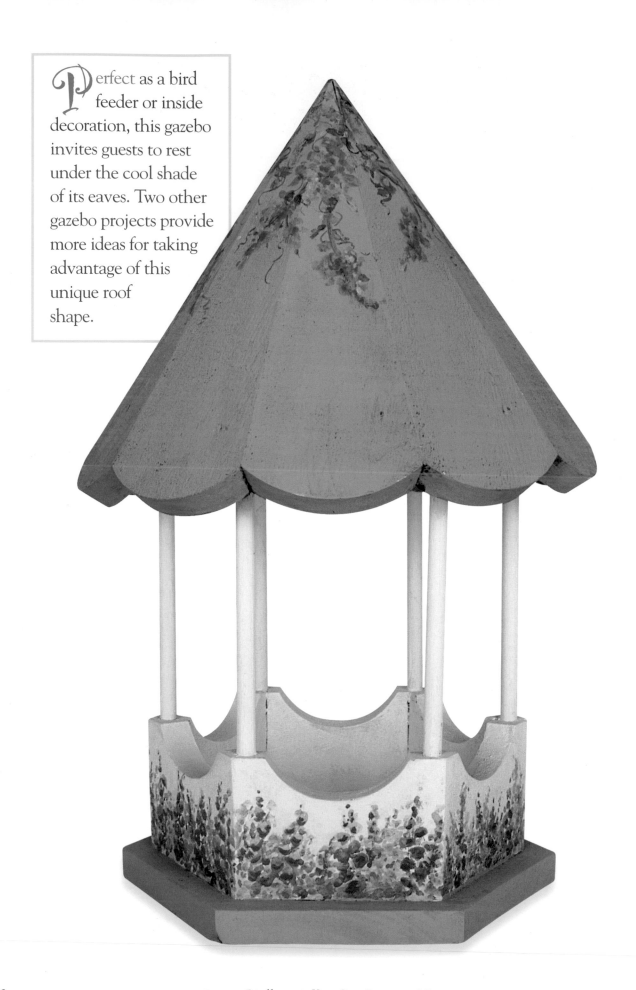

erfect as a bird feeder or inside decoration, this gazebo invites guests to rest under the cool shade of its eaves. Two other gazebo projects provide more ideas for taking advantage of this unique roof shape.

# Pastel Gazebo

## 1 Basecoat

Basecoat the gazebo Titanium White. Paint the roof with Green Mist and the base with Ice Blue.

**Sample project colors.** pink flowers: wash of Antique Rose, shaded with Alizarin Crimson and highlighted with Antique Rose + White; purple: wash of Summer Lilac, shaded with Pansy Lavender and highlighted with Lilac; yellow: wash of Golden Straw, shaded with unthinned Golden Straw and highlighted with Yellow Light; blue: wash of Salem Blue, shaded with unthinned Salem Blue and highlighted with Salem Blue + White.

**Wisteria** (bottom left): Use thinned Burnt Umber on liner brush to establish vine. Use corner of no. 6 brush with Summer Lilac and Lavender to establish shape and placement of flowers. Shade with Pansy Lavender. (bottom right): Highlight flowers with Lilac. Paint leaves with Forest Green. Add more vines with Burnt Umber. Add light leaves with Forest Green + White and Hauser Light Green.

## 2 Paint Flowers and Foliage

Paint the flowers with a dabbing motion, laying in a middle value, then

To paint the foliage, begin with Avocado at the bottom, working into lighter values with Hauser Light Green. Leave openings for the flowers. Establish flower shapes with a wash of the middle color value.

Highlight with the lightest flower value.

## 3 Paint the Wisteria

adding shading with a darker value. Highlight with the lightest value. Many different color combinations can be used.

Add shading to the flowers with a darker value.

Add centers to the flowers with Golden Straw, highlighted with Yellow Light.

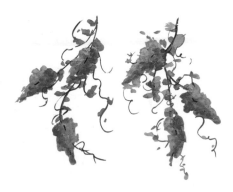

Only the bravest birds will venture into this house, which uses crackle medium to create an aged, weathered effect. This project also shows how to make windows to suit any birdhouse.

# Haunted House

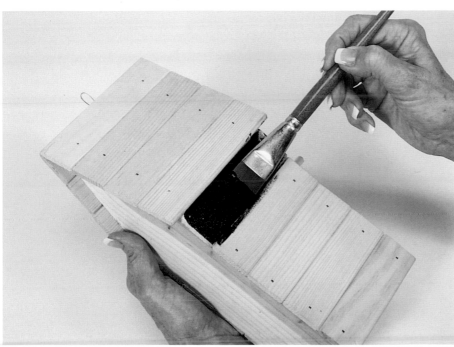

## Materials

- craft store birdhouse
- ½" x 1" welded wire: 6-square piece
- chimney cutout
- craft sticks
- DecoArt Weathered Wood Crackle Medium
- wire cutters

*DecoArt Americana acrylic paints*
- Lamp Black
- Soft Black
- Black Plum
- Dove Grey
- Neutral Grey
- Royal Purple
- Ice Blue
- Yellow Green
- Burnt Umber
- Evergreen
- Titanium White

*Delta Ceramcoat acrylic paints*
- Lime Green

*Apple Barrel acrylic paints*
- Midnight Blue

*Brushes*
- 1" synthetic flat or 1" sponge
- no. 2, 6 and 8 flats
- no. 0 liner
- no. 0 round detail
- ½" rake

## 1 Basecoat

Sand the house well and wipe with a tack cloth. Basecoat the house with Lamp Black. Let dry.

## 2 Apply Crackle Medium

Following manufacturer's directions, apply crackle medium over the basecoat. Let dry for the manufacturer's recommended time.

## 3 Apply the Top Coat

Mix equal parts of Dove Grey and Neutral Grey. Apply a heavy but even coat over the crackle medium.

### Hints For Using Crackle Medium

Apply crackle medium with a fan brush or sponge brush. Apply a generous amount of medium, but not so much that it runs and drips. Check the surface occasionally as it dries and gently wipe away runs and drips that may occur. Apply medium quickly. Do not overwork it. The less you work with it, the better it will crackle. When applying the top coat, avoid repainting the same areas because the paint may lift or smear. Allow to dry.

Quaint Birdhouses You Can Paint and Decorate

## 4 Basecoat and Paint a Shingled Roof

Basecoat the roof with Black Plum. When dry, lightly draw shingle rows with a pencil. Use a rake brush to shade under each row of shingles with Soft Black.

## 5 Highlight the Shingles

Use a rake brush to highlight the bottom of each row with Royal Purple.

## 6 Outline the Shingles

Use thinned Royal Purple on a liner brush to loosely outline the rows and define a few shingles.

### 1. Cut the welded wire windows

Use wire cutters to cut the welded wire. After the basic cuts are made, trim away any points that stick out so that edges are as smooth as possible. Note: In the materials list and throughout the step-by-step instructions, the term "4-square" or "6-square" is used to indicate a section of welded wire that contains four or six squares.

### 2. Draw the windows

Use the welded wire as a pattern to draw the outline of the window, then paint the window. Allow to dry before gluing the wire in place.

### 3. Cut shutters

Use the welded wire as a guide for cutting craft stick shutters to the right size with pruning shears or a craft knife.

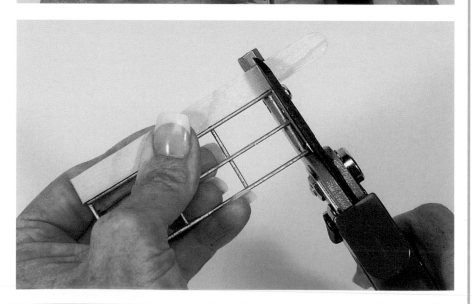

Quaint Birdhouses You Can Paint and Decorate

## 7 Make the Windows

Cut a 6-square piece of welded wire for the window. Use it as a guide to draw a window shape on one side of the house. Paint the window with Lamp Black.

## 8 Cut and Paint the Shutters

Use shears or a craft knife to cut 3-inch long shutters from craft sticks. Paint the shutters Royal Purple. Paint the inset panel shapes with Black Plum, then shade them with Soft Black.

## 9 Paint the Ghosts

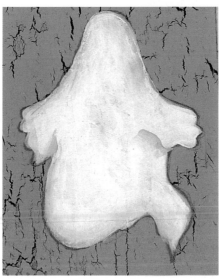

Basecoat the ghosts with Titanium White. Shade with Ice Blue.

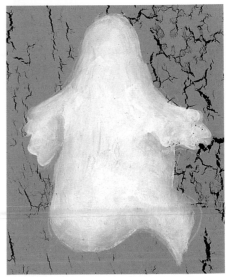

Darken the shading with Midnight Blue + Titanium White.

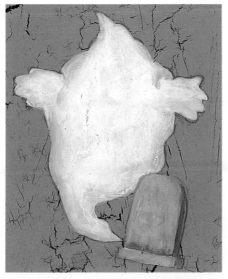

Paint the tombstone with Titanium White + Lamp Black.

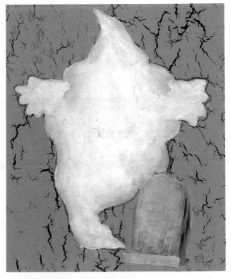

Highlight the tombstone with a wash of Yellow Green.

## 10 Paint More Ghosts

Outline ghosts with thinned Midnight Blue. Draw face details, outline the tombstone and do the lettering with a permanent black pen. Pull up grasslike strokes with Burnt Umber and Evergreen. Finally, paint the bat with Lamp Black and a spider web with a black pen.

## 11 Paint the Chimney

Basecoat with Soft Black. Use short strokes with a no. 8 brush to make bricklike shapes with Neutral Grey.

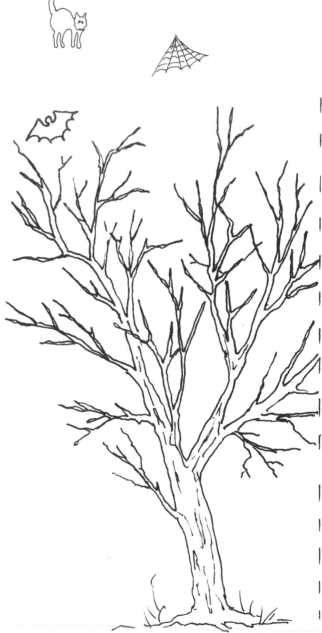

Quaint Birdhouses You Can Paint and Decorate

## 12 Paint the Tree

Paint the tree with Soft Black. (If Soft Black is unavailable, a mixture of Lamp Black + Burnt Umber may be substituted.) Use an up-and-down motion with the chisel edge of a no. 6 flat to paint the trunk of the tree and the largest branches. Paint small branches with a liner brush.

## 13 Final Touches

**Cat.** Paint the cat Lamp Black. Highlight the face, back and tail with Dove Grey. Paint the eyes Lime Green. **Roof.** Paint holes in the roof with Lamp Black. To make the holes more distinct, highlight the edges with Royal Purple. **Bats.** Paint the bats Lamp Black. The eyes on the bat and the eyes peering out of the roof holes are Lime Green.

**Windows.** Glue the welded wire window and shutters to the side of the house. Glue one shutter slightly askew so it looks as though it is hanging loose from a broken hinge.

**Spider webs.** Use thinned Lamp Black on a liner brush or a black permanent pen to draw spider webs under the eaves and at the top of the shutter.

The A-frame birdhouse turned cabin can make a cozy fireplace addition. Making the log siding is easy—just press twigs into mortar patch. Rusty tin completes the look.

# Hunting Lodge

## 1 Stain the Roof

Mix Driftwood and Cranberry Wine on the palette. Thin the paint with water and apply a light wash of color to the roof.

## 2 Cut the Logs

To make the logs, choose sticks that are as straight as possible and approximately ¼- to ⅜-inch in diameter. Trim away knobs and side branches. Measure each twig against the section of the house it will cover, and mark the length with a pencil. Where logs meet at a corner, allow ½-inch excess so that back logs will intertwine with the side logs. Logs under the A-frame eaves that do not intertwine with others at the ends should be cut to fit. Use pruning shears to cut enough sticks to cover the front, back and sides of the house.

## 3 Apply the Mortar

Spread the mortar over one side of the house at a time. Start on the back of the house to get the feel of working with the materials. Use a small trowel to spread mortar patch approximately ¼-inch thick so that it will hold the logs when they are pressed into it.

## 4 Add the Logs

Starting at the bottom of the house, gently press each log into the wet mortar patch. Leave one stick width between the logs so they will alternate with the side logs rather than join in a continuous line. Repeat until all sides of the house are covered.

## 5 Finishing Touches

Use a nail to make a small hole in each tin cutout. Attach them to the house with glue and small nails.

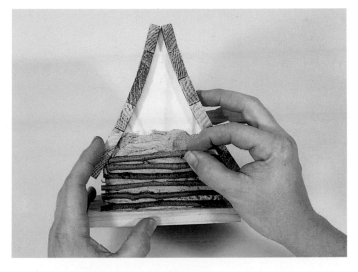

Press the twigs into the mortar patch.

### Materials

- A-frame birdhouse
- premixed concrete and mortar patch
- ten or twelve long, thin, straight twigs
- rusted tin: trees and moose cutouts (available in craft stores)
- painting knife or small trowel
- small nails

*DecoArt Americana acrylic paints*
- Driftwood
- Cranberry Wine

*Brushes*
- 1" synthetic flat or 1" sponge

H ave fun with the tent shape of this birdhouse—the possibilities are endless. On this "camping" tent, simple wood cutouts, twig fishing poles and green moss accessorize the playful shape.

GONE FISHING

# Camping Tent

## 1 Sponge the Tent

Sand the birdhouse well and wipe with a tack cloth to remove dust particles. If the birdhouse wood has a prominent grain pattern, basecoat the house with Khaki Tan before sponging. Squeeze Raw Sienna, Honey Brown and Antique White onto the palette. Wet the sea sponge. Squeeze it as dry as possible. Dip the sponge into Honey Brown. Sponge the paint onto the birdhouse, almost covering the surface.

Sponge with Honey Brown.

Sponge Raw Sienna over Honey Brown.

## 2 Add More Colors

Follow the procedures as in step one to sponge Raw Sienna over the Honey Brown. Use heavier pressure on the sponge, twisting and turning it on the surface to blend paint to look like suede. Sponge lightly with Antique White in the same way. Buff the surface lightly with a dry-wiped sponge. Let dry.

## 3 Paint the Tent Stakes and Flap

Basecoat the stakes with a wash of Burnt Umber. Overstroke with Raw Sienna. Use straight Burnt Umber to shade and separate the sticks. Paint the tent flaps Antique White, shaded with Burnt Umber. Shade the tent under the flaps with Burnt Umber. Use a liner brush with thinned Burnt Umber to outline the edge of the flap. Paint the opening with straight Burnt Umber.

## 4 Finishing Touches

**Canoe.** Basecoat the canoe with Antique White. Add shading and stitching lines with Burnt Umber.

**Trees.** Paint the trees with Evergreen and the star with True Ochre. Use a liner brush to outline the trees and star with thinned Burnt Umber.

**Sign.** Paint the "Gone Fishing" sign with Buttermilk. Sponge the edges with Evergreen. Letter the sign with a black permanent pen. Drill holes in the sign. Thread wire through the holes for hanging.

**Final assembly.** Cut twigs and glue together in a pile. Cut long thin twigs for the cane poles. Glue the canoe, miniature oars, logs and cane poles to the front of the tepee. Tuck moss around the base and glue in place. Hang the fishing sign on a small nail and glue to secure.

---

### Materials

- tent-shaped birdhouse
- sea sponge
- drill with 1/16" bit
- small nails

*DecoArt Americana acrylic paints*
- Eggshell
- Honey Brown
- Raw Sienna
- Antique White
- True Ochre
- Evergreen
- Buttermilk
- Burnt Umber
- Khaki Tan (optional)

*Brushes*
- no. 2, 6 and 8 flats
- no. 0 liner
- no. 0 round detail

---

### Optional Accessories

- one 1/2" fish-shaped wood cutout
- 20-gauge wire
- canoe cutout
- miniature oars
- twigs for logs and cane poles
- green moss

utout patterns for the snowman and pine tree are included with this project, but you'll find a variety of wood shapes to choose from at your favorite craft store. Any wood cutout can be charmingly embellished with a bit of paint and scrap fabric.

# Snowman Cutout House

## 1 Preparation

To make the windows, cut two 4-square pieces of ½" x 1" welded wire. Cut four 2¼-inch window shutters from jumbo craft sticks. Cut trim pieces to fit under front eaves from ¼-inch wide basswood strips. Round front edges of wood cutouts by sanding the edges with a sanding block or palm sander.

## 2 Basecoat

Sand the house and trim pieces. Wipe with a tack cloth to remove dust particles. Basecoat the house with Midnight Blue. Paint the roof, shutters, trim strips and snowman cutout with Light Buttermilk. Paint the tree cutouts Hauser Dark Green with Burnt Umber trunks.

Round the front edges of wood cutouts by sanding the edges with a sanding block or palm sander.

### Materials

- craft store birdhouse
- wood cutouts: two trees, one snowman
- chimney-shaped wood cutout
- two jumbo craft sticks
- ½" x 1" welded wire: two 4-square pieces
- ¹⁄₁₆" x ¼" basswood strips
- DecoArt Snow-Tex
- wire cutters
- 20-gauge wire
- drill with ¹⁄₁₆" bit
- jute twine
- scrap of fleece or flannel for hat
- ½" x 6" strip of plaid fabric
- upholstery foam

*DecoArt Americana acrylic paints*
- Light Buttermilk
- Burnt Umber
- Hauser Dark Green
- DeLane's Cheek Color
- Tangelo Orange
- Lamp Black

*Apple Barrel acrylic paints*
- Midnight Blue

*Brushes*
- 1" synthetic flat or 1" sponge
- no. 2 and 8 flats
- no. 0 liner
- fan

## 3 Paint the Checkerboard Roof

Cut a ⅝-inch square sponge from upholstery foam. Wet the sponge, then squeeze it dry. To check spacing of checkerboard pattern, place the sponge on the top left corner of the roof and mark along the side lightly with a pencil. Move the sponge over one square and make another mark. Continue until the top row is marked. Adjust placement of squares if needed. Squeeze Midnight Blue onto the palette. Dip the sponge in the paint, blot the sponge on the palette to remove the excess paint and to distribute the paint evenly. Sponge the checkerboard pattern on the roof, reloading the sponge as needed.

## 4 Paint the Snowman

To paint the detail on the snowman, use a dry-wiped brush to add blush to the cheeks with DeLane's Cheek Color. Paint the nose with Tangelo Orange. Draw the mouth, eyes and buttons with a permanent pen or Lamp Black. Stencil or paint the hearts on the shutters and on the snowman with DeLane's Cheek Color.

## 5 Finishing Touches for the Snowman

**Arms.** To make the arms, cut a 3½-inch length of 20-gauge wire. Fold the wire in half and twist the halves together, leaving ½-inch untwisted at the ends for the hands. Repeat for the second arm. Drill holes in either side of the snowman. Insert and glue the folded ends of the wire in the holes.

**Hat.** To make the snowman's hat, cut a 1¼" x 2¼" piece of fleece. Fold a ¼-inch cuff on one long side and glue to secure. Glue fleece around the snowman's head. Use a single strand of jute twine to tie around the top of the hat.

**Muffler.** To make the muffler, cut a ½" x 6" strip of plaid fabric and tie it around the snowman's neck.

Use a square sponge to create a checkerboard pattern on the roof. Keep turning your hand to vary the pattern of the squares.

Make wire arms for the snowman.

Quaint Birdhouses You Can Paint and Decorate

## 6 Paint the Trees
Use a fan brush to apply the Snow-Tex to the trees.

## 7 Finish the Birdhouse
Glue the snowman and trees to the front of the house. Glue the wire windows and shutters to the sides of the house. Brush Snow-Tex on the perch, the bottom edge of the hole, the roof, the windows and the snowman's hat and arms.

Apply Snow-Tex to the trees with a fan brush.

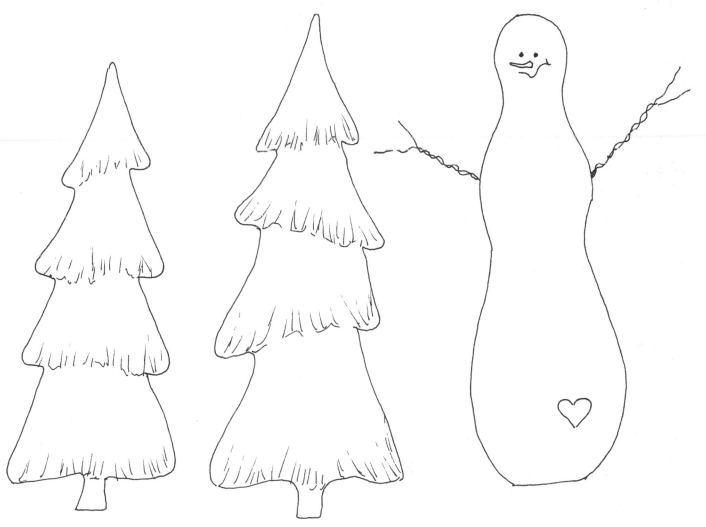

Patterns for wood cutouts.

*T*he chilly onset of winter is given perfect dimension on this house with decorative snow. Spatter the house with Titanium White to get into the snow-falling spirit of the season.

# Painted Snowman House

## 1 Preparation

Cut two 6-square window frames from welded wire. To make the shutters, cut craft sticks approximately 1⅛-inch long.

## 2 Basecoat

Sand the house well and wipe with a tack cloth. Basecoat sides of house with Midnight Blue. Paint roof with Khaki Tan. Paint shutters Deep Burgundy.

### Materials

- craft store birdhouse
- ½" x ½" welded wire: two 6-square pieces
- craft sticks
- wire cutters
- upholstery foam
- DecoArt Snow Tex

**DecoArt Americana acrylic paints**
- Khaki Tan
- Burnt Umber
- Raw Sienna
- Deep Burgundy
- Ice Blue
- Red Iron Oxide
- Tangelo Orange
- Lamp Black
- Titanium White

**Apple Barrel acrylic paints**
- Midnight Blue

**Delta Ceramcoat acrylic paints**
- Copan Blue

**Brushes**
- 1" synthetic flat or 1" sponge
- no. 2, 4, 6 and 8 flats
- no. 0 liner
- fan

## 3 Paint the Shingled Roof

Lightly draw the rows of shingles with a pencil to check spacing. Use slightly thinned Raw Sienna + Burnt Umber on a liner brush to paint the rows of shingles. Keep linework sketchy and irregular, adding a few vertical lines to suggest individual shingles. Shade under each row with Raw Sienna. Redefine linework if necessary.

## 4 Paint the Brick Chimney and Base

To paint the bricks on the chimney and base, basecoat the areas with Khaki Tan. Cut a ¼" x 1¼" piece of foam. Squeeze

Deep Burgundy and Midnight Blue onto the palette. Use Burgundy, Red Iron Oxide, Khaki Tan and Midnight Blue sparingly. Dip sponge randomly into the colors, and blot it on the palette to remove excess and soften the colors. Lay the sponge horizontally on the basecoated surface, making a row of bricks. (Vertical lines will be added later.) Skip a narrow space for mortar and lay the sponge on the surface again. Repeat for each row, reloading the sponge as necessary. Use a liner brush to add the vertical mortar lines with Khaki Tan.

# 5 Paint the Snowman

Basecoat the snowman with Titanium White.

Shade around the edges with Burnt Umber. Basecoat the hat with Lamp Black.

Paint buttons, mouth and eyes Lamp Black. Use Tangelo Orange shaded with Burnt Umber for the nose. Highlight hat with Titanium White. Basecoat the muffler Deep Burgundy. Highlight the hat with Titanium White.

# 6 Finish the Details

**Muffler.** Overpaint the muffler with Deep Burgundy + Titanium White. Shade with Deep Burgundy + Lamp Black. Use thinned Ice Blue for the stripes and fringe. Paint the tassel with Raw Sienna. Shade with Burnt Umber.

**Arms.** Paint branch arms with Burnt Umber.

**Tree.** Use the chisel edge of a brush to paint the tree trunk and birdhouse pole with Burnt Umber, shaded with Burnt Umber + Lamp Black.

**Birdhouses.** Use the chisel edge of a brush to paint the birdhouse poles with Burnt Umber, shaded with Burnt Umber + Lamp Black. Paint the birdhouses Titanium White. Use Deep Burgundy for one roof and Copan Blue for the other.

## 7 Add the Snow

Use Titanium White to paint snow on the tree branches, the rooftops of the birdhouses, the snowman's hat and arms and the ground around the snowman and trees. For more dimension, use a fan brush to apply Snow-Tex to the base, roof and top of the chimney. Spatter the house with Titanium White.

ecause the house was made of rough cedar, it has the look of stucco when painted. If your house has a smooth surface and you want to add texture, follow the directions for the stucco finish on the bank.

# Christmas House

## Materials

- cottage-style birdhouse
- DecoArt Snow-Tex

*DecoArt Americana acrylic paints*

- Eggshell
- Santa Red
- Golden Straw
- Moon Yellow
- Hauser Light and Dark Green
- Burnt Umber
- Glorious Gold
- Neutral Grey
- Driftwood

**Brushes**

- 1" synthetic flat or 1" sponge
- no. 2, 6 and 8 flats
- ½" or ¾" flat
- no. 0 liner

*Optional accessories*

- ½"-wide artificial garland
- strand of miniature lights
- ⅛"-wide red satin ribbon
- miniature basket and pot of poinsettias
- miniature gifts

### 1 Basecoat

Only very light sanding is needed because of the rough texture of the house. Wipe with a tack cloth. Basecoat the house, chimney and base with Eggshell.

### 2 Stain the Roof

Because of the warm tone of the wood, the roof was left unpainted and was used as the middle value of the shingles. Only the shading (dark value) and highlight (lightest value) tones are painted. To paint the roof, double-load a ½- or ¾-inch brush with Burnt Umber on one half and Moon Yellow on the other. Pull horizontal strokes across the roof to create rows of shingles. Darken the Burnt Umber shading if needed.

### 3 Paint the Windows

(see below)

### 4 Paint the Stones

To make the stones on the chimney, base and corners, use a no. 6 brush. Squeeze puddles of Neutral Grey, Driftwood and Eggshell onto the palette. Dip the brush into Neutral Grey and Driftwood. Press the brush on the surface to be painted, making irregular stone shapes. Leave spaces between the stones for mortar. If stones seem too dark, pick up Eggshell with the other colors.

### 5 Decorate the House

Paint the door Santa Red. Paint the wooden frames of the window panes with Burnt Umber. Apply Snow-Tex to the roof and base. Glue ½-inch garland and miniature lights under the eaves. Form a wreath of ½-inch garland for the door. Add a red ⅛-inch wide ribbon bow. Use a miniature basket and gifts on either side of the door and poinsettia-filled flowerpots at the corners.

Paint the window areas with Golden Straw. Overstroke with Moon Yellow. Paint the window trim with Hauser Dark Green.

Use the chisel edge of a no. 6 brush to pat a tree shape with Hauser Dark Green. Highlight the branches with Hauser Light Green.

Paint the garland with Glorious Gold. Use the handle end of the brush to dot ornaments with Santa Red.

The top of this bird-house could be painted with many different color combinations. Choose three values of colors to match your decorating theme.

# Flower Shop

## Materials

- 6-sided birdhouse with base
- wood cutouts for steps

### DecoArt Americana acrylic paints
- Eggshell
- Hauser Dark Green
- Hauser Medium Green
- Hauser Light Green
- Reindeer Moss
- Lilac
- Orchid
- Lavender
- Royal Purple
- Black Plum
- Cadmium Yellow
- Yellow Light
- Light Buttermilk
- Dove Grey
- Terra Cotta

### Brushes
- 1" synthetic flat or 1" sponge
- no. 2 and 6 flats
- no. 0 liner
- no. 0 round detail

## Optional Accessories

- two 1" candle cups
- two ¾" candle cups
- two ½" wooden flowerpots
- three 1" grapevine wreaths
- miniature watering can and trowel
- small artificial and dried flowers
- green moss
- two wood cutouts for signs:
  ⅝" x 1⅜" x ⅛"
- small twig

## 1 Basecoat the House

Lightly sand the house and wipe with a tack cloth. Because the shading and highlighting are applied "wet-on-wet," basecoat one or two sections at a time with Hauser Dark Green; move on to steps 2 and 3 before basecoating the next section.

## 2 Highlight

While wet, use long vertical strokes of Hauser Light Green and Reindeer Moss in the middle of the section.

## 3 Shade

Shade the edges with Hauser Dark Green. Paint all sides and let dry.

Quaint Birdhouses You Can Paint and Decorate

## 4 Basecoat and Shade the Roof

Draw a light line approximately 2 inches below the tip of the roof. Leave the area above this line unpainted. Basecoat a few sections of the roof with Orchid. While wet, use Lavender to shade around the tops and sides of the petals. Pull a few short shading strokes down into the petals.

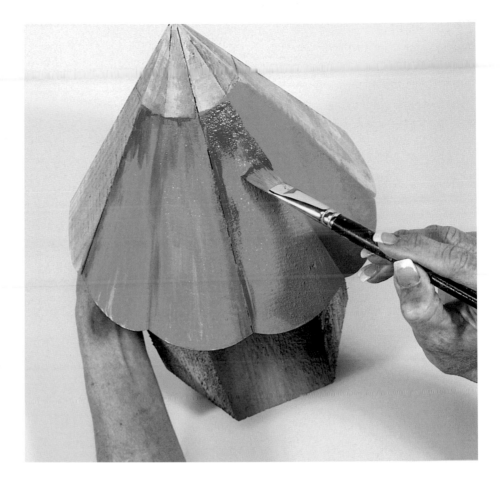

## 5 Highlight the Roof

Highlight the bottom of each petal with Lilac, pulling the strokes up into the petal. Repeat these steps until the roof is covered.

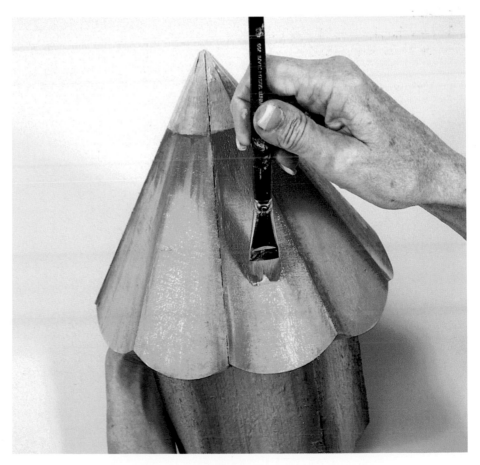

## 6 Basecoat and Shade the Flower "Center"

Basecoat the top 2 inches of the roof with Yellow Light. Use the corner of a no. 6 brush in a patting and sliding motion to shade around the edges of the center with Cadmium Yellow.

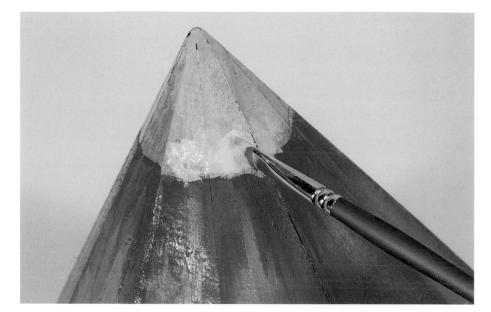

## 7 Add Darker Values

Strengthen dark values around the edges of the center with Black Plum.

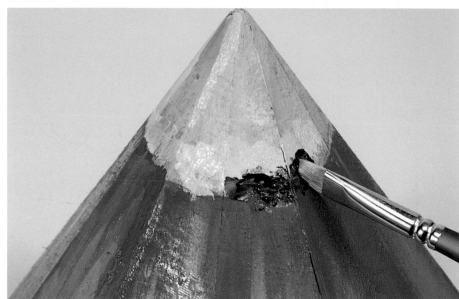

## 8 Highlight Center

Highlight the top of the flower center with Yellow Light + Light Buttermilk, using the same patting and sliding motion.

Quaint Birdhouses You Can Paint and Decorate

## 9 Add Additional Highlights

Use a liner brush to pull lines of thinned Black Plum from the center down into the petals.

## 10 Paint the Door and Base

Lightly draw the outline of the door with a pencil. Paint the base, steps and door with Dove Grey. Paint a Royal Purple border around the door.

## 11 Paint the Signs

Basecoat the signs with Dove Grey. Paint the lettering and trim with Royal Purple. The flowerpot is Royal Purple shaded with Black Plum and highlighted with Lilac. The topiary is Hauser Medium Green shaded with Hauser Dark Green.

## 12 Add the Accessories

**Candle cups.** Paint the 1-inch candle cups with Royal Purple. Paint the ¾-inch candle cups with Dove Grey, then paint a design by using a liner brush to make squiggly lines of Royal Purple.

**Flower pots.** Paint the wooden flowerpots with Terra Cotta.

**Topiary.** To make the topiary, roll green moss into a ball, using hot glue to hold it together. Cut a 2-inch length of a small twig for the stem. Fill the other pots with dried or artificial flowers and greenery, and glue to secure.

**Wreath.** Decorate one of the grapevine wreaths with dried flowers. Hang the wreath over the perch, and glue to secure. Attach other wreaths to the side of the house with glue and small nails.

**Final steps.** Glue the flowerpots, watering can and trowel in place with craft glue.

Sign patterns.

*A* white picket fence is the perfect addition to this proper Victorian bird dwelling, complete with a birdhouse of its own!

Quaint Birdhouses You Can Paint and Decorate

# Victorian Spring Cottage

## 1 Basecoat the House

Basecoat the house with Pink Quartz. Shade with Wild Rose under the eaves. Paint the roof with Blue Wisp.

## 2 Paint the Door and Windows

Transfer the pattern shown on the right, adjusting the size to fit your birdhouse. Paint the door Wild Rose. Paint the windows with a wash of Drizzle Grey. Use White to paint tieback curtains in the windows and door. Paint the trim around the door and windows with White. Draw

### Materials

- craft store birdhouse
- two 1½" wooden heart cutouts

*Delta Ceramcoat acrylic paints*
- Pink Quartz
- Wild Rose
- White
- Blue Wisp
- Drizzle Grey
- Lilac
- GP Purple
- Azure Blue
- Dark Jungle Green
- Black Green
- Apple Green
- Blue Mist
- Bonnie Blue
- Dark Forest Green

*Brushes*
- 1" synthetic flat or 1" sponge
- no. 2, 6 and 8 flats
- no. 0 liner
- no. 0 round detail
- bristle fan

a scalloped design above the door, around the hole and under the eaves. Use slightly thinned White on a liner brush to paint the design. Dip the handle end of the brush into White and use it to make round "knobs" on the trim. Outline the white trim with a black permanent pen.

## 3 Paint the Hearts

Basecoat the heart cutouts with White. Use thinned Blue Mist on a liner brush to do cross-hatching on the hearts. Base in the shape of the flowers with Pink Quartz. Shade the flower with Wild Rose. Paint the stems and leaves with Dark Forest Green, highlighted with Apple Green.

## 4 Paint the Flowers

Use the corner of a no. 6 brush to paint the flowers. Thin the paint for the first applications of color. Begin with Dark Jungle Green at the bottom. Apply the paint with a patting and sliding motion, varying the amount of pressure on the brush to create light and dark values. Leave openings for the flowers. Pick up Apple Green as you work into lighter leaves. Strengthen the color near the base with a few touches of Black Green. Use a

liner brush to make upward strokes with Dark Jungle Green for the flower stems. Paint the flowers with a dabbing stroke, working from dark to light. Use GP Purple and Lilac for the purple stalks. Use Azure Blue + White for the blue flowers. Add more White for a lighter value. Paint a few stalks of White, using a touch of Bonnie Blue for shading.

### How to Add a Fence

If you want to add the base and picket fence, cut ½-inch thick wood 1-inch larger all around than the house. Glue the house to the base so that the back is flush with one edge of the base with a 1-inch margin on each side and a 2-inch margin in front. Glue the fence to the base. The picket fence was purchased from a craft store.

Add interest to a plain gazebo bird feeder with commercial patching compounds that are available at most home improvement stores.

Concrete patch creates a thatched roof while popcorn ceiling patch adds texture and dimension to the flowers.

# Textured Gazebo

## Materials

- gazebo-style bird feeder
- premixed concrete and mortar patch
- premixed popcorn ceiling patch
- painting knife or small trowel

*DecoArt Americana acrylic paints*
- Titanium White
- Hauser Dark Green
- Hauser Light Green
- Avocado
- Black Green
- Deep Burgundy
- Berry Red
- Coral Rose
- Gooseberry Pink
- Khaki Tan
- Driftwood
- Neutral Grey

*Brushes*
- 1" synthetic flat or 1" sponge
- no. 6 synthetic flat
- bristle fan

Spread mortar at least ⅛-inch thick so you will be able to create texture with a fan brush.

**1 Basecoat**
Sand the gazebo and wipe with a tack cloth to remove dust particles. Paint the sides, inside and outside, with Titanium White. Leave the roof and base unpainted.

**2 Texture the Roof**
Work on two or three sections at a time. Apply concrete and mortar patch evenly to the roof with a painting knife or small trowel.

## 3 Add Interest to the Textured Roof

Use a bristle fan brush to push the mortar into evenly spaced rows by pressing into the mortar with a light upward pressure. This will make a small ridge in the mortar. Rows should be ½ to ¾-inch apart. Repeat on all sections until the roof is covered.

## 4 Paint the Roof

When the mortar is dry, basecoat the roof with Hauser Dark Green.

Quaint Birdhouses You Can Paint and Decorate

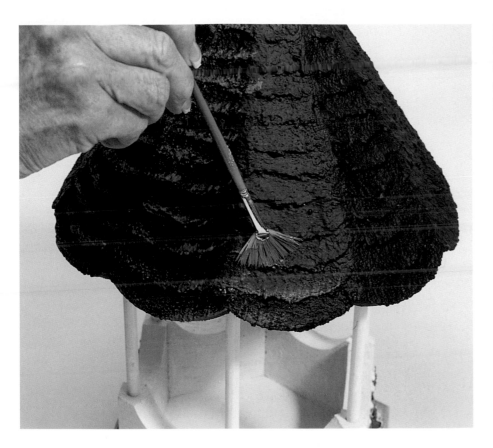

## 5 Highlight the Roof

Use the fan brush to highlight each ridge with Avocado. Apply paint sparingly with an upward motion of the brush.

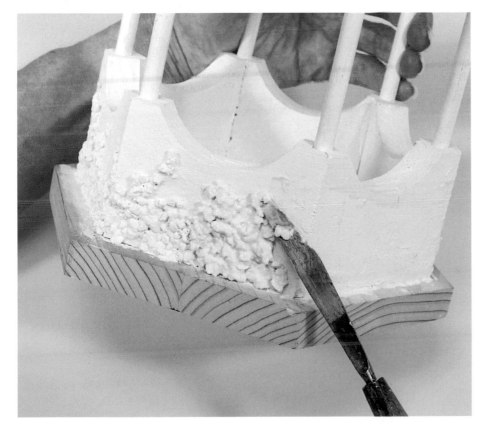

## 6 Apply the Popcorn Patch

To create the texture for the flowers, use a painting knife or small trowel to apply popcorn patch to the sides of the gazebo. Start near the base, applying enough patch for good coverage. Form an irregular edge at the top to suggest stalks of flowers. Let dry before painting.

## 7 Paint the Dark Foliage

Use a patting motion with the corner of a no. 6 brush to paint the foliage and flowers. Work from dark to light. Paint the foliage with Black Green nearest the base, then work upward into Hauser Dark Green.

## 8 Paint Lighter Leaves

Work into Avocado and Hauser Light Green as you paint the top foliage. Paint irregular edges at the top to form varying heights for the flowers. Let dry.

Quaint Birdhouses You Can Paint and Decorate

## 9 Paint the Flowers

Use the same technique to paint the flowers. Paint a dark value with Deep Burgundy. Work into Berry Red for a middle value. Use Coral Rose and Gooseberry Pink for the lightest values. Add more leaves around the flowers if needed. As paint dries, the colors will darken, so more highlights may be needed.

## 10 Paint the Base

Paint the base with Neutral Grey, Khaki Tan and Driftwood. Use the brush to apply colors randomly with a patting and sliding motion, picking up first one color, then another. Blend only slightly so the base resembles marble or cement.

Use Deep Burgundy for dark values, Berry Red for middle values and Coral Rose and Gooseberry Pink for the lightest values. Reapply the lightest color for more "sparkle."

**Fishing Lodge**

This rustic lodge is well suited for outdoor use, even though it is decorated with all kinds of miniatures and trimmings. On houses that will be outside and exposed to the elements, use a quality brand of clear, long-lasting silicone sealant to glue the accessories to the house. For example, the stone chimney was built with aquarium rock held in place with 35-year silicone. All surfaces should be covered with varnish that is especially formulated for outdoor use. Created by Retha and Pete Potter.

### Lighthouse

Guide the ships to port or simply use this lighthouse as a night-light. An old glass insulator, available from antique shops and flea markets, holds the beacon light. The lamp can be wired with an electric cord or battery-powered fixture. Be sure to use low-temperature bulbs for safety reasons. Created by Retha and Pete Potter.

# Gallery

***Red Barn***
There are several ways to obtain a rustic, aged look on birdhouses built from rough wood. One is by using a dry-brush technique. The house is basecoated with a color, then another color is applied with only a minimum amount of paint on a dry-wiped brush so that both colors are visible, creating the look of a surface that has worn and aged through several coats of paint. When applying the top coat, use very light pressure on the brush so that the paint only catches on the raised grain, leaving the basecoat showing in the recessed areas. Created by Retha and Pete Potter.

## Old Shoe

Build a birdhouse for the old woman who lived in a shoe. Change a plain birdhouse into a shoe shape with an oval bentwood or papier maché box. Simply find a box that fits the size of the house and cut off one end. To make the sole, cut a base of thin wood slightly larger than the outline of the house and the box.

# Gallery

### Gingerbread House

This house is an example of letting imagination soar. Change a plain craft store birdhouse into a whimsical gingerbread house. Basecoat the house a warm gingerbread color. Paint Christmas candy trim with acrylic paints. Frost the chimney with tinted Liquitex Gelex topped with a wood bead painted as a cherry. Paint dots and lines of "frosting" with iridescent fabric paints. Use mushroom pegs, painted to resemble M&Ms, to decorate the roof and painted gingerbread boy wood cutouts to guard the door. Add a dusting of glitter paint and your birdhouse will look good enough to eat! Created by Billee Jennings.

Quaint Birdhouses You Can Paint and Decorate

**Americana House and Fun House**
Add a bit of fun and whimsy to your village with the Americana House and
Fun House. Add cute ball feet to the Fun House with ⅞" wooden balls.

# Source List

The raw birdhouses used in this book were purchased from the following manufacturers. If your local craft and hobby stores don't carry the design you're looking for, contact these companies for more information.

**Walnut Hollow**
(800) 950-5101
Woodcraft products available nationwide at leading craft and department stores.

**Add Your Touch**
P.O. Box 570
Ripon, WI 54971
(414) 748-6777
A complete mail-order line of kit and assembled birdhouses, also available at craft stores.

**Something Different**
P.O. Box 52174
Tulsa, OK 74152
Mail-order glue injectors (for structural paint) and handmade wooden birdhouses shown on 82, 106 and 114.

- **vinyl screening:** hardware and building supply stores

- **welded wire:** hardware and farm supply stores

- **craft sticks:** (Popsicle sticks) and **jumbo craft sticks** (larger version of craftsticks): craft supply store

- **upholstery foam:** fabric and upholstery stores (make-up sponges may also be used)

- **aquarium rock:** small rocks sold in pet stores or in large discount stores where pet supplies are sold

- **silicone sealant/glue:** found in building supply and home improvement stores. Be sure to choose the kind that dries clear.

- **shingles:** found where doll house supplies are sold. To make your own shingles, select cedar with a straight, even grain. Decide on the size of each shingle, usually about ⅜-inches wide and 1-inch long. Cut the cedar across the grain to the desired size. Secure the wood in a vise and use a wood chisel to chip the shingles from the wood piece.

- **wood cutouts:** craft store. To make substitutes for birdhouses to be used indoors, cut shapes from light- or medium-weight cardboard (not corrugated).

- **cinnamon sticks:** craft store or spice shop

- **basswood or balsa strips:** craft or hobby store

- **miniatures:** craft store, or where doll house supplies are sold

# Index

# Index